Enough!

Learning to Survive and Thrive in Brokenness

Endorsements

The story you are about to read lays bare the soul of a very painful personal journey. Seldom will you encounter such an honest and probing assessment of brokenness and the intervening grace of God. The pain of a childhood without its expected joys and freedom. The crushed hopes, dreams, and deep wounds of being used and cast aside as a young adult. The growing strength that only a loving Savior can grant in an environment of total despair. Our heavenly Father snatched Diana from the abyss of depression and defeat. He began to build wholeness and peace into her broken life—a process that continues to this day. Jesus has not made her strong in her own abilities. Rather, he has become her strength and has used her broken life to keep her dependent upon him. Triumph and peace are found in the Savior. Walk in Diana's steps as you turn the pages of this book and learn of the One who redeems when all seems lost.

—**Dr. Edgar Hardesty,** Retired Professor of Bible, Archaeology and Jewish Studies, Cairn University, Langhorne, PA.; Pastor Redeemers Fellowship, Shrewsbury, PA, Speaker

God once gave me a front-row seat to a friendship between two remarkable girls. Joni had been a talked-of high school athlete. Now, after a diving accident, she faced what seemed a barren landscape of lifelong paralysis. Diana was her effervescent Christian friend who dropped out of college to

help Joni down the early miles of that daunting path. I knew Diana when she was *the* primary spiritual influence in Joni's life. What I did not know was the litany of private sufferings Diana had endured that had so shaped her character. She tells her story here—my good friend who first introduced me to Joni, and to whom I owe a great deal.
—**Rev. Steve Estes**, Author, Speaker, Senior Pastor Brick Lane Community Church, Elverson, PA

Paul writes in 2 Corinthians 1:3–4: "Blessed be the God and Father of our Lord Jesus Christ, the Father of mercies and God of all comfort, who comforts us in all our tribulation, that we may be able to comfort those who are in any trouble, with the comfort with which we ourselves are comforted by God."

Diana Mood has skillfully and graciously turned the trying experiences of her life into a book that shares with the reader the comfort with which she herself is comforted by the Father of mercies and the God of all comfort.

With frankness she shares heartaches that allow us to fully appreciate the depth and intensity of the Lord's comfort to his loved ones when they are put to trial, sometimes in the most unexpected ways.

In this book you will find not only one woman's life story, with all the ups and downs common to all, but you will find a journal of how the Lord Jesus Christ encourages and sustains his own and turns their most difficult trials into an opportunity to show his unmatched love.
—**Rev. G. W. Fisher**, President, Western Reformed Seminary Board, Board Member, Presbyterian Union Mission, Senior Pastor, Tacoma Bible Presbyterian Church, Tacoma, WA

Why read this book, you ask. The content of its pages represents seventy years of neglect, abuse, dysfunction, and disappointment, followed by sorrow, heartache, and deep pain. Is it possible that you will become numb and weary of such a story? You may think the writer has little reason for hope. What kept me from putting the book down, however, was not so much the author's many tales of heartache, but the focus of her persistence.

No matter the nature or frequency of pain, Diana Mood never wavered in her focus or love for her Lord. This story is about a person who has learned how to embrace the Gospel regardless of the pattern of pain and sorrow that would overwhelm anyone. It is a story of true hope.

—**Chuck Garriott**, Executive Director and Founder of Ministry to State, Washington, DC

Jesus said to abide in him. Without him, we can do nothing. This memoir tells the story of a woman who believed that. She knew, apart from Jesus, she could accomplish nothing. Whatever she did, she talked to God about it and trusted in him for answers. She did not give up. It's a story about a woman who lived her life for Jesus. Was she perfect? Not hardly, but she learned to trust in God, not in people or things. She lived by example. Through faithful trust in her Lord and Savior we see the resilience God gave her. Whatever we do, the results are not up to us. They are up to God. This story demonstrates that.

—**Carol P**, head writer, artist, teacher, and retired ombudsman

After I read Diana's memoir, I was inspired to prepare and preach a message on Psalm 34:19. "Many are the afflictions of the righteous, but the Lord delivers him out of them all." Diana, thank you for telling your own story and reminding us that we're not alone in the journey of life.

—**Neamen Mesgina**, Development Consultant, Co-Founder and former Vice President of The Global Transformation Network. Inc.

I met Diana at a conference some years ago and then had the opportunity to see her and Terry in action, training a team of coworkers in Argentina about community development focused on disabilities. As a regional leader, I needed people like them, with passion and experience, to help our team move to new territory, and their contribution to our ministry was significant.

What I did not take the time to do, was to find where all this strength, passion, and knowledge was coming from. I had heard bits and pieces of their testimonies during lunches and breakfasts together, but very seldom did I have the chance to see the full picture of who was joining my table, all the wounds, the learning experiences, the great and the low moments, and this book provides that background understanding. Great servants of God are made of deep, transforming stories, of which Diana has much to tell.

Diana opens up to show everyone what made her story— the good, the ugly, the questionable, the mistakes, and the challenges. At points you may find her pain hard to bear, and you can tell she is not sugar-coating the narrative, even when she is looking for God´s answers. She also provides a good description of what is it like to be the one walking alongside those that live with disabilities, and how dependence happens both ways. Her story uncovers the emotional nudity of someone left with empty spaces when unable to perform acts of service she used to live by. And there is Jesus, to collect the broken pieces and rebuild, once and again. You see, this is also his story, and how the truth of who we are in him becomes our complete health, in a journey of ongoing learning and experiencing his life-giving presence.

—**Alexandra Bibi MacLeod**, Resource Facilitator for Disaster Preparedness and Response, Medical Ambassadors International

After living through the last forty years with Diana's wounds, tears, and grief—past and present—you, like I, will discover the severe mercies with which God has gifted her. Her transparent authenticity enables us to share her intimacy with her Savior, the scriptural principles by which she lives and grows into the likeness of Christ and gains confidence in how he made her. With the forgiveness process, Diana is

blossoming. It's been my unspeakable joy to be her friend and walk with this godly woman for forty years. She will impact your life too.
—**Terry Graham**, Co-Founder and former President of Global Transformation Network. Inc.

I thought I knew my friend of fifty years until I read this book! I couldn't put it down! The ever-ready-to-help, fun-to-be-with, encouraging Christian girl who would always listen, and who would drive two hours to help me in a crisis, had never revealed all that made her who she is ... until now.

It is a great blessing to see in Diana's life how God uses the circumstance of our lives to shape us and bring us to himself.
—**Bonnie Heppe Fisher**, watercolor artist, Legacy Publishing Group

This book reveals God's love in new ways bringing meaning and purpose within a difficult journey. A lifetime of struggles, tragedies, and trials can't stop Diana from her commitment and passion for following Jesus. Though tempted to give up numerous times, Diana continued to choose to press into her Savior, Jesus Christ, and thus she experienced light in darkness, hope in despair, and encouragement in depression—being supported by dear friends along the way. In everything, God receives the glory. He is the One who brings blessing from brokenness.
—**Bob Reusser**, Former Director of Navigators Encore Mission

What an honor to hear your story! Knowing you makes the story all the more God glorifying. It is a real story. It is a poignant story. One that has that power to bring healing to others. Thank you for sharing it with me.
—**Sundee Simmons**, Associate Director, Perspectives Service Office Team, Perspectives Global Network

Many people think that those God uses in a mighty way must come from functional, Christ-honoring families and lead a charmed life. But that is not normally the case. God

uses broken vessels for his glory each and every day. As it says in Romans 5:3–5: "but we also rejoice in our sufferings, because we know that suffering produces perseverance, perseverance, character and character, hope. And hope does not disappoint us because God has poured out His love into our hearts by the Holy Spirit, whom He has given us" (NIV). Diana is a living example of those verses. Through the pain and suffering in her life, God has brought forth many fruitful things. I have had the privilege to call her friend and mentor for twenty years. Amid her personal struggles, she introduced me to ESL (English as a Second Language) Ministry. While in pain herself, her constant encouragement and dedication to the vision of ever-expanding ESL ministry within the PCA and beyond has certainly been a factor in the establishment of Mission to North America's ESL ministry and its ever-growing impact on churches nationwide. May this book encourage all those going through difficult times. As Diana does, know that God is present in your pain. You are not alone. God is enough and his purposes will still be accomplished.
—**Nancy Booher**, Ministry to North America, Presbyterian Church in America, ESL Ministries Director

As I read through her life, I was constantly reminded of Paul's words that we have this treasure in jars of clay. Hers is a very human, and at times difficult, story of generational brokenness, but at the same time it is a rich testimony to God's patient care for one of his children. Another Scripture that comes to mind says, "We are perplexed, but not in despair." She has indeed lived an amazing life.
—**Al Englar**, Mission Director, The Navigators

Diana. Just finished reading your book. I'm amazed at your incredible memory. Thankful for your journey and your openness to share your struggles and hopes. You take me back to my childhood. I too grew up in Lochearn and went to Campfield. My sixth-grade teacher also had an important role in my life. I was two years ahead, graduating in 1965 from Woodlawn. I love how you share your deep friendship with Terry. I am sure many people will benefit from all your experiences. Especially your desire to trust the Lord through so much turmoil. I will reread your book tomorrow. There is so much to take in. Thanks for sharing your journey and your vulnerability. Love and admiration.

—**Linda Reinhold**, wife and ministry partner of Chuck Reinhold, retired Young Life Director in MD and NY, founders of Young Life Ethiopia

In sharing the deepest secrets of her life, Diana Mood has given her readers a precious gift, reminiscent of Laozi's words: "Whoever is capable of knowing when they have had enough will always be satisfied." After reading *Enough,* I think you'll agree that the Old Irish word *tánaic* beautifully describes the journey that has been her life: "She has arrived." Save room on your Keepers Shelf for this one, because you'll want to read it again ... and again!

—**Loree Lough**, *USA Today* bestselling author of 130 award-winning books.

Enough!

Learning to Survive and Thrive in Brokenness

Diana Mood

ELK LAKE PUBLISHING INC

PUBLISHING THE POSITIVE
Plymouth, Massachusetts

COPYRIGHT PAGE

Enough! Learning to Survive and Thrive in Brokenness

Cover and Interior Design: Derinda Babcock
Editor: Paul Conant, Deb Haggerty
Author Photo: Dawn Kearney

PUBLISHED BY: Elk Lake Publishing, Inc. 35 Dogwood Dr. Plymouth, MA 02360, 2021

LIBRARY CATALOGING DATA

Names: Mood, Diana (Diana Mood)
Enough! Learning to Survive and Thrive in Brokenness

250 p. (6 x 9 in.)

Identifiers: ISBN 13: 978-1-64949-379-8 (paperback) | 978-1-64949-380-4 (trade paperback) | 978-1-64949-381-1 (e-book)

Key Words: rejection, low self-esteem, forgiveness, hope, personal growth memoir, perseverance, spiritual growth.

Library of Congress Control Number: 2021946012 Nonfiction

DEDICATION

This is a true story. Thank you to all the family and friends, named and unnamed, who helped me find my way to knowing and loving God by knowing and loving me.

TABLE OF CONTENTS

FOREWORD

Before You Begin …

Over the years, I have written countless articles, many books, and a few forewords, but none like this one. The following paragraphs mirror personal reflections I've never quite expressed on paper before. So, before you go further, just know that I'm a little biased about the author.

That's because Diana Mood saved me.

I do not mean she scraped me off the pavement from despair and self-destruction; rather, she constantly pushed and prodded me to take seriously the lordship of Christ in my life—especially after a devastating accident in which I broke my neck. Diana was always *there*. Whether skipping a college semester to shepherd me through dreary months in a hospital or serving years as my trusted caregiver after I left rehab, the sacrifices she made were enormous. I admired that about her.

She was like that, even back in tenth grade when we met in high school biology. Diana possessed a sharp-edged intellect. A rigorous love of God. A robust knowledge of the Bible. A wacky sense of humor. And an enormous capacity to care. I could write reams on that, but on the following pages, perhaps you'll see it yourself.

Suffice it to say, Diana made my life as a paralytic fun, filling it with zany escapades and adventures that would now be considered dangerous. We were faith pilgrims together, braving uncharted questions about God posed by my wheelchair. She helped create the musical score of my life which included hymns, high school chorales, and the occasional Beatles hit. She made my paralyzed life meaningful with late-night discussions and debates over books and ideas. In all this, not once did she allow self-pity to rule my day. Perhaps that's how she indeed saved me.

We were the best of friends. Which is why—and this is the hardest part—I grieve over this touching memoir. For the most part, her path through life is pitted with profound suffering. Not the sort of suffering I endured with a broken neck. Hers is a much harder affliction. Wounds and gashes that rip holes in the heart. Brutal emotional injuries that leave one reeling. And here's the hard part: much to my regret, the choices I made for my own future only hurt her further.

But this is not why you should read her memoir. This isn't for the voyeuristic. You should read it because we are all in need of pushing and prodding. Your life journey may not be like Diana's or mine, but if you are honest, you will often feel blindsided by suffering. You will have unyielding questions about God. Your expectations will be crushed, and you too will lick the wounds of your emotional injuries. You *may* even allow a little self-pity to creep in.

Do not allow yourself to go down that dark, grim path. The book you hold in your hands is your husky, brave-hearted guide through affliction. Its pages may be splattered with pain, but you will find on them eternal principles from the mouth of God himself. For the One who carried Diana these many decades is none other than Jesus, the Man of Sorrows acquainted with grief. So, take your favorite coffee to your easy chair and get started reading. Be moved. Be helped. Be inspired.

For you, too, may need a little saving.

Joni Eareckson Tada

Joni and Friends International Disability Center

2020

ACKNOWLEDGMENTS

This is not a tell-all book, but almost. While all the stories are true, some names and identifying details have been changed or omitted to protect the privacy of the people involved. Numerous stories went missing on the cutting room floor.

Special thanks to Sue Kline, editor extraordinaire. Scribblings of a novice became an intricate tapestry of engaging characters woven into the tangled web of my life. Thank you, Joyce Sackett, for introducing us. Thanks to Loree and Larry Lough for introducing me to Elk Lake Publishing.

Thanks to caring family and friends—you know who you are—who lovingly endured my first visceral efforts. A shoutout to my sisters for detailed edits and formatting corrections. And for reliving the most outrageous memories, sharing countless tears, and raucous laughter. A gold star to Terry, a forever friend, who prayed me across the finish line.

Labor of love fails to describe the internal pain I relived typing these words on these pages. Why do it? Because the life I have lived flows through God's fingertips before it reaches me, for his glory, my good, and yours.

Blessings on you as you read it.

PART ONE

CHAPTER 1—HOUSE ON FIRE

I was five when I began to dream about running into burning buildings. I would suddenly become aware of black smoke billowing onto the street from open windows, and tongues of hot, bright flames leaping through the roof and shooting high above the other homes in my neighborhood. I always knew who the fiery house belonged to, and I instinctively ran toward the danger to rescue them.

Upon waking, I never remembered how, but I always managed to save my neighbors. We would emerge from the inferno like Shadrach, Meshach, and Abednego in the Bible, unsinged and unharmed. *What was all that about,* I'd ask myself, as similar dreams continued throughout grade school.

Loud voices often roused me from my childhood sleep. My parents were arguing. The intensity would rise and fall, punctuated by screaming and crying. I would lie motionless on their double bed, temporarily paralyzed by fear, murmuring inaudible pleas for them to stop, please stop. Eventually their voices became more muffled, and I could drift back to sleep. I would eventually be transferred to the living room sofa for what remained of the night. We lived on the third floor of a ramshackle, one-bedroom row house near the Pimlico Race Course on the western edge of Baltimore City. It was 1952.

The night terrors eventually escalated into weekend suitcase packing. The contentious arguments began on Friday evenings when my father returned home from work. Mom would vent her frustrations and demand that he change his ways or else she was leaving and taking me with her. That was my cue to pack my little suitcase with a few items of clothing and wait for her to grab my hand and march down the stairs. Dad watched in tears as Mom and I walked a few doors down the street to spend the night at Vanessa's row house. She was one of Mom's friends and had a daughter, Judy. I enjoyed spending time with her.

On Saturday evenings, after he returned home from work, Dad would always plead with Mom to come back to him. He'd vow to be different, more loving, more attentive. Sadly, he wanted to change, but he didn't know how. Still, we would return home. This drama continued for two years with several variations. I liked to stay with Aunt Margarette, my mother's older sister, and my cousins, who lived a few more blocks up the hill.

I continued to dream about running into burning buildings.

I am a child of ill-equipped parents who themselves were born into less-than-ideal circumstances.

While still in the womb, my mother, Mary, managed to survive when her drunk father threw her mother, Rosie, down a flight of stairs. At age seven, my mother mercifully lost her dad to a massive heart attack. The physical mayhem ended, but Rosie was no match for my strong-willed, rebellious mother. Out of desperation, Rosie often locked Mary in her room or threatened to tie her up to keep her out of mischief.

Mom pranked the neighbors, routinely spent dental check-up money at the movies, experimented with smoking cigarettes, and liked to jitterbug—a scandal in those days and in her conservative neighborhood.

My father's early years were strained by an alcoholic father's binges and physical abuse. John was ashamed of his immigrant parents, which may have intensified his introversion. I never heard him talk about any friends from his neighborhood, school, or military days. It seemed he didn't know how to make or keep friends. Yet he had great potential; he was intelligent and motivated and had a wonderful tenor voice. And he had dreams for himself, his marriage, and his children.

Mom was sixteen and Dad was barely twenty-two when they met at a neighborhood church. He was very handsome, and she was well-developed for her years. Dad had recently returned from serving as a staff sergeant in the South Pacific during World War II. They married quickly. Both wanted to escape their parents' homes, but they were penniless and had to live with Mom's mother, Rosie, until Dad found a job. Their first apartment was in Baltimore City. Cheap, dumpy, unfurnished, but theirs. Eleven months later, I was born. Mom was ill-equipped to be a mother—still a child herself.

We moved seven times in my first seven years. Our tiny, rat-infested apartments were always near family on Baltimore's western edge, and we always had a roof over our heads. I didn't have a bed or a room until we finally moved to Lochearn in Baltimore County when I was seven. My first bed came from Grandmother, and the dresser was a sawed-off bottom set of drawers from her old china closet.

Mom's protests continued to morph over time. Leaving on the weekends hadn't worked and took a lot of effort and planning. Maybe yelling louder or getting more physical would get the desired results. Arguments at the dinner table began at normal volumes. Mom's voice would rise and fall and then gradually crescendo at various tempos, punctuated by staccato-like utterances, followed by accusations hurled in sustained screaming. She would pound on Dad's chest with both fists, maybe slap him across the face, until he was able to grab her wrists to protect himself. When I was unable to tolerate the fighting any longer, I would insert myself between them, one hand shoving Mom and the other shoving Dad, like a referee separating boxers and forcing them into their corners for time out. The tangled struggle would continue for several moments until Mom finally backed away, reaching for an object to throw.

On one memorable night, a dozen eggs hit the wall. Another time, a plate full of spaghetti smothered in tomato sauce splattered all over the kitchen. Dad's army training was useful when ducking incoming projectiles. I became clever at timing the precise moment I should intervene to avoid the mess on the wall and end the combat. These scenes always ended with Mom's tears, my fears, and Dad's helpless frustration. He didn't know how to handle this childish woman who made demands he didn't comprehend and couldn't satisfy. My mother was desperate for affection and romance, fighting for love she could *feel*, like that of Clark Gable and Vivien Leigh in *Gone with the Wind* and Humphrey Bogart and Ingrid Bergman in *Casablanca*. Longing for glamour and stylishness, she could strut like Marilyn Monroe and radiate like Grace Kelly. She was all allure and glitz. Dad looked like a movie star, but he had no clue how to feed her fantasies, nor did he want to.

Mom didn't like being poor. This wasn't how her life was supposed to go. The life she desired meant marrying a handsome guy who swept her off her feet, made big bucks, and bought her lots of stuff. It meant having a beautiful baby girl who she named after a famous teen singing sensation, Deanna (Diana) Durbin, and living happily ever after in suburban luxury. Her reality was starkly different. Many weeks we didn't have money for food, and various family members graciously dropped off a few bags of groceries. Mom couldn't bear to see me dressed in rags, so she routinely charged what she couldn't afford. Soon the debt was unmanageable, which only made things worse. For several years, Dad worked three jobs on the weekends without sleeping. Monday mornings, he would go back to his primary job, work all day, and then sleep. He was basically absent from my life, trying to earn enough money to pay the clamoring creditors. He cut the grass, took out the garbage, and often went food shopping after working fifteen-plus hours. I never heard him complain.

Mom was home, alone, with me. Unhappy. Constantly angry. Bored. She never showed interest in doing things with me. She seldom helped me with anything, not even homework. I suspect she felt inadequate, never having graduated from high school. She didn't sew, wasn't a very good cook, and didn't play board games. No visiting museums, reading books to or with me, going to lectures, or even going to the movies together. She arranged things to keep me occupied that did not require her presence or participation. But we did enjoy singing together at the piano.

Christmas Eve, Dad and I would bundle up and go hunting at nearly empty Christmas tree lots for the annual Charlie Brown look-alike. We set it up together. Then it was my job to make it beautiful, and I did. On a few memorable Christmases, Dad surprised me with presents I especially wanted—a tape recorder, a Yamaha guitar, a used spinet piano, a bike, a set of Britannica encyclopedias, and a used car when I turned sixteen. I don't remember ever buying him anything on Christmas, Father's Day, or on his birthdays.

My daytime thoughts were being stalked by a grotesque monster disguised as a soothing balm for whatever distress was assaulting my emotions.

"Hi, Mom, I'm home," I yelled as I bounded through the kitchen screen door after walking home from school. "Got anything good to eat? I'm famished!"

"Look in the fridge, you'll find something," she said.

I was eleven. Sugary snacks were favorites—ice cream, Tastykakes, candy, milkshakes. Popsicles were best on hot days like this one. I hurriedly grabbed several, pulled out my high-chair-like metal chair, and parked it and myself in front of the TV. I rotated the back panel over my head and, voila, it became a tray for whatever I was munching. Thirds and fourths were routine as I watched *The Lone Ranger* followed by *The Roy Rogers Show*, *Lassie*, and other favorites. Happily singing along with the theme songs, I stayed enthralled until dinner time, which meant macaroni and cheese, spaghetti with a few meatballs, or pasta and ground beef goulash.

TV was more than escapist, after-school entertainment, however. The large wooden box with the tiny glass screen became my window to the world. Daily news programs like *The Today Show* with Dave Garroway and *The Huntley-Brinkley Report* told stories of what was happening around the world. I inhaled attention-grabbing stories watching original combat footage from World War II and similar historical programs. I was sick at home the day of Kennedy's assassination in 1963, and remained glued to the TV screen for days until his burial at Arlington Cemetery.

My interest in history and current events was nurtured by watching TV. As my reading improved, I devoured books from the school library and looked for opportunities to discuss my thoughts and impressions about everything and anything with adults in my life. Yes, I was a couch potato with an addiction to empty calories causing an expanding waistline. But my world was also expanding.

I gawked at Elvis Presley's gyrating hips as he sang "Hound Dog" on Ed Sullivan's variety show in 1956. The extended family gathered at Aunt Marg's house for that one. She had a new color TV, and we were in awe the whole hour. We all gathered again in November that year to watch *The Wizard of Oz*. My spirits were lifted by the songs and characters, and I sang myself to sleep many nights dreaming of bluebirds and rainbows, being carried far away from the chaos at home.

CHAPTER 2—IT'S A GIRL!

Grandmother beamed and said, "It's a girl!" as she got off the phone with Dad.

"Yippie, yippie! It's a girl! It's a girl! Yippie, yippie!" I exclaimed as I ran around the house full of joy. "When can I see her? When is she coming home? I can hardly wait!"

On September 12, 1957, after almost nine long years, I finally became a big sister. Her name was Jessie.

I became an experienced diaper changer, bottle feeder, sour spit-up and stinky mess wiper-upper after two years of daily childcare responsibilities. When Cassie was born on February 27, 1959, it was like living the movie *Ground Hog Day*. Surprise, excitement, and joy all over again. We were a family of five now, tucked into a small home in a middle-class neighborhood.

I wanted to be a big sister, but became a surrogate mother. Old issues remained: debts multiplied, expectations went unmet, and demands increased on the adults in the house. Mom's "It's all about me" behavior and her continuous melodrama permeated every corner of our lives and home. Although she loved us, the message was not getting through to me or these two beautiful, sweet little sisters.

Dad was now a self-employed piano tuner working from 10:00 a.m. to midnight, but the debt Mom continued to pile up was more than he could manage alone. Mom found a full-time job close to home from 4:00 p.m. to midnight as a telephone operator at Sinai Hospital where she eventually became a supervisor. I had to come home right after school to fill in the parenting gaps while they worked. Warming up dinners Mom left. Helping with homework. Supervising bath time. Putting the girls to bed. Separating them when they were locked into hair-pulling combat. Mom had the backyard fenced in and bought a boxer puppy we named Heidi. She became a ferocious watch dog who protected us from occasional Peeping Toms and petty thieves. In 1967, Dad had a prefab room added onto the back of the house for his piano workshop, and Mom borrowed money from a friend for an in-ground, fiberglass and concrete swimming pool with a diving board in the backyard. If we had to be home alone at least we would be safe and happily occupied in their absence, or so she thought.

CHAPTER 3—FIGHTING FIRES WITH LOVE

Whatever my childhood lacked in other areas, it was rich in spiritual mentors who saw my distress and reached out to offer me security and a sense of belonging.

I distinctly remember sitting on Grandmother's lap in her bedroom as she read to me the crucifixion story of Jesus from Gustave Dore's book of black-and-white engravings that illustrated many Bible stories. Sensing my distress, Grandmother urged me to invite Jesus into my heart. I did, and the love of Jesus immediately filled my young heart and began to calm my fears. I knew I could trust him even when my parents seemed out of control.

The church fellowship hall was full of colorful posters depicting the life of Christ. My favorite was called *The Lost Sheep* by Alfred Soord and was based on a story Jesus told in Matthew 18:12–14. Jesus is clothed in shepherd garb and clinging to the edge of a steep precipice, fully stretched out with his right hand inches away from grabbing a terrified lamb that had drifted away. I could imagine that lamb bleating, "Jesus, I'm over here, over here. Help! Help! Rescue me! Please." In the story, Jesus rescues the desperate creature and ends the parable by saying, "And if he finds it, truly I tell you, he is happier about that one sheep than about the ninety-nine that did not wander off" (v. 13).

I had been the lost sheep. Jesus had rescued me. He rejoiced over rescuing me, more than all the others left behind in safety, contentedly chomping grass in the pasture. I felt swaddled in his loving embrace whenever I looked at that poster—safe in his arms, close to his heart.

Verses in attractive calligraphy also decorated the walls at church. My favorite was Matthew 7:12: "So in everything, do to others what you would have them do to you, for this sums up the Law and the Prophets." I yearned to model my life after the Jesus I loved and knew in these and many other verses from the Bible. I knew my grandmother and aunts and uncles tried to live like that, but they were adults. I was a kid. I had a lot to learn.

Dad faithfully drove us to Sunday school and church each week at the South Baltimore Bible Presbyterian Church on South Hanover Street. Mom and Dad argued the whole way, plastered on smiles upon arriving, and then resumed bickering when back in the car. But they managed to be civil with each other when we went out to dinner with extended family, who picked up our tab. These were cherished moments of peace and rest in my otherwise daily diet of full-throated arguing.

Church was family, literally and figuratively, from cradle roll to age seventeen. Grandmother, Aunt Marg, Uncle Dick, cousins Carole and Rachel, and other aunts, uncles, and cousins shepherded me through the tumultuous years of my childhood. They loved me with extraordinary love, and for this I am forever grateful.

By far, my two favorite days at church were Christmas Day and New Year's Eve.

Christmas Day rituals began with opening one present, usually the biggest. The rest would wait until we returned from church. Bundled in coats, hats, scarves, gloves, and boots, we left home at 5:30 a.m. for the 6:00 a.m. candlelight Christmas caroling around the church neighborhood. Regardless of weather or temperature, we went block to block singing favorite carols at each stop concluding with "We Wish You a Merry Christmas!" We circled back to church chilled to the bone but happy to put our stocking feet on the steamy radiator as we giggled and anticipated breakfast in the fellowship hall. The refreshments were impressive: assorted warm buns and donuts from the corner bakery, tea and coffee in china cups, colorful linen tablecloths, and napkins. Breakfast was followed by the 8:00 a.m. candlelight service. After the concluding prayer, all the children would dash along the center aisle eager to get home and open the rest of their presents.

I tore into all my presents by noon and wrapping paper was strewn helter-skelter. Aunts, uncles, and Grandmother filled the gaps with their gifts and minimized poverty's impact. Always surprised, my simple longings were satisfied by treasures discovered under the spindly, tinseled tree. I usually brought one gift to play with, and off we drove to Aunt Marg's house for our clan gathering and a scrumptious Christmas dinner of roasted turkey, glazed ham, and all the trimmings: German potato salad, candied yams, stuffing with gizzards and caramelized onions, cranberry garnish, and homemade cookies, cakes, and pies. Oh, the mouthwatering aromas that greeted the senses when we skipped through the front door!

Bear hugs and kisses received, I hurried to be seated at the large table. Uncle Dick said the blessing, and the feasting began. Dishes passed in both directions, accompanied by a cacophony of loud, simultaneous cross-table conversations punctuated by giggling, laughter, and love. It was chaos, but we loved it. This Smith clan was famous for it. We lingered long, delaying the trip home until more bear hugs and "I love yous" were generously given and received by all. It was a genuine Norman Rockwell event we all still remember with fondness and nostalgia. Peace and joy permeated the day, pushing back the shadows and burning buildings of the night.

New Year's Eve was another special time at church. The evening began with dinner around crowded tables in the upstairs hall. Christmas lights and decorations still framed the three large windows looking out onto the dimly lit sidewalk and asphalt. Christmas lights shone back into our fellowship hall from adjoining, marble-stooped row houses, making the whole scene picturesque. Long tables covered with white linen tablecloths each boasted a festive centerpiece. We always had party hats and paper horns. Chairs carefully placed between the tables left enough room to squeeze into your seat next to your best friend, your cousin, or your gray-haired grandmother with her holiday hat festooned with long feathers. Tea in china cups with saucers, bite-size sandwiches, petit fours, decorated Christmas cookies, and treats of all sorts greeted us. Happy chatter indicated how glad we were to spend the evening with folks we knew and loved.

Eating was followed by a service in the worship center downstairs. We tightly packed ourselves into the old wooden pews. The hymn sing began with people shouting out page numbers from the dog-eared hymnals, vying to have their favorite sung next. Together we made a joyful noise in four-part harmony. A few folks had professional-quality voices. A retired military trombonist and Aunt Blanche, the pastor's wife, at the grand piano accompanied our melodious efforts, and our spirits lifted heavenward in unity as the final moments of the outgoing year came to an end.

Various ones stood up and gave testimony to how God had blessed them or sustained them through the past year's trials and tribulations. Dr. Slaght, our pastor, shared a passage of Scripture, and then small, white candles with cardboard collars were handed out as we all stood in a circle around the large room. Each person passed the tiny flame until all the candles were lit. Our collective glow illuminated the room as the ceiling lights went dim, mimicking the eternal light we had inside—Jesus: the way, the truth, and the life. At midnight, we spontaneously sang "Blest Be the Tie That Binds."[1] We all knew the words by heart. Often my eyes filled with tears.

$$\mathcal{D}$$

Rev. Slaght held my attention as his tall, imposing frame rose from the pulpit chair. Left hand holding his open, well-worn Bible, the right gesturing with alternating authority and sensitivity, he could pull you into a message with a voice that filled the hall with its deep tones. His storytelling was animated, and he used the whole platform to engage us. He could be timid or fearless, loud or hushed, awed or incredulous. He was skillfully captivating minds and hearts as he radiated genuine love, compassion, and concern for all of us. He longed for us to comprehend God's Word and be touched by its divine truth.

I was captivated by his teaching and leaned forward on the edge of the pew, eager to hear the end of the story or to fully understand the nugget of truth he vividly painted, always wanting to hear and know more. My lifelong pursuit to know God is deeply rooted in the seeds of his preaching. My lonely hours were filled with discovery and excitement as my capacity to study and reason grew. I was motivated to find answers to the questions he had stirred in my soul. His gift to me remains precious beyond measure.

Then there was Mrs. Slaght, our pastor's wife. I called her Aunt Blanche. She wasn't my biological aunt; she was Uncle Dick's older sister. (Dick married Aunt Marg, Mom's sister.) Hard to follow, I know, but that connection was an important link in our family's future and to one of the most important influences in my young life.

Blanche was way ahead of her time. She had studied journalism and photography, was an accomplished pianist, dabbled in writing, and created 3-D dioramas for commercial store windows. She had a flair for drama, art, cooking, and sewing. It seemed as if she knew how to make and do anything—all done with passion and enthusiasm.

She's a big reason vacation Bible school is among my best childhood memories. She made sure each year was laced with adventure around themes like Champions for Christ, Pioneering with Christ, and Defenders of the Faith. Our days were filled with dramas, parades, costumes, reel-to-reel movies dramatizing Paul's missionary journeys, Scripture-memorization competitions, singing, pantomimes, and many other wonderful events pouring from Aunt Blanche's storehouse of children's treasures, costumes, and creativity.

She had four great loves: Jesus; her brother, Dick; her husband, Arthur; and people, especially children. Although she had three stepchildren, whom she loved dearly, she had none of her own. Aunt Blanche looked for potential in all children. She envisioned success and achievement for each one and provided opportunities for them to learn and experience the joy of succeeding at a task.

I was blessed to be one of those children. She treated me like I was special and could be counted on to be responsible with any assignment she gave me.

"Diana, you oversee the book table this week. Check the box next to a book title when it is borrowed and check the box again when it is returned. You can do it."

"Your lovely voice is perfect to sing this solo with the ensemble. Here are the words. Practice is Wednesday evening. See you then."

"The part of the oldest daughter in the Thanksgiving pageant was written with you in mind. Ask Grandmother to make you a Pilgrim frock."

She reinforced qualities she intuitively saw in my character, and they thrived in the nurturing embrace of her affirmations.

I developed confidence in myself and competence in a variety of areas under her influence. But most importantly, she modeled integrity, enthusiasm, commitment, and enjoyment in small things. For instance, she kept many scrapbooks of favorite things, one of which was poems clipped from newspapers and magazines. After her passing, I inherited these small treasures saved over a lifetime: recipes, jokes, short stories, skits, and personal Bible studies. She scattered all sorts of precious scrip scraps along the paths of others to spice things up and brighten their lives.

Many people stood to tell their stories of how Blanche blessed their lives at her memorial service. Neighbors comforted after losing loved ones. Grandchildren well-loved and pampered. Young adults inspired to set goals and achieve them, and on and on.

Aunt Blanche loved well, spread joy, used her gifts to maximum benefit, and allowed life's ups and downs to make her wiser and godlier. She was one of the best role models I ever had.

In 1960, the Mid-Atlantic Bible Presbyterian Churches launched a youth program called 20th Century Overcomers.[2] Leaders within the denomination wanted to inspire its young people to grow in the knowledge of their faith and to prepare them for meaningful service in advancing God's kingdom. One strategy for reaching that goal was to hold summer camps and snow conferences for kids from all the churches within a local presbytery. Many talented and gifted pastors, teachers, missionaries, elders, and change-makers emerged from the fun, fellowship, and instruction at Overcomers' events. They remain active all over the world as ambassadors for Christ in their spheres of influence.

As the blazing campfire shot hot embers into the cool night air at the Overcomers summer Bible camp in the

Poconos in August of 1962, my heart responded to the speaker's challenge to dedicate my life to serving God, to making a difference in the world by giving him my all. Silently, solemnly, I made a vow, *Here I am, Lord, take me.*

I was thirteen.

PART TWO

CHAPTER 4 – INSTANT CELEBRITY AT CAMPFIELD ELEMENTARY

I attended Campfield Elementary after we moved to our small single family home in the suburbs. I made a smart decision right away. I found the music teacher and auditioned for the choir. I made it! And when he found out I also played the piano fairly well, he asked me to accompany the choir on one song at the upcoming fall concert.

"Sure. That would be fun," I said.

The choir was center stage on two rows of risers. I was seated at the piano, stage left, facing the audience. The heavy stage curtains were closed, hiding us from the audience. No one had noticed the curtains were tangled up in the rear piano wheels. When the stagehands heard the conductor tap his baton on the music stand, they began to pull the ropes to open the curtains. Simultaneously, as I started to play the intro, the choir began to sing, and the piano started to move sideways. Not to be undone by the situation, I stood up and kept playing the piano until the stagehands noticed what was happening and stopped pulling the ropes. One of them came onstage and placed the piano bench under me, and I finished the piece.

I became an instant celebrity when the audience roared with applause, whistling and belly laughing at the whole scene.

As a celebrity I had no trouble finding friends to sit with during lunch, the big social hour of the day, and I relished the popularity. Yet, I kept noticing a handful of kids who sat silently at the ketchup and mustard table, seeming lost and alone. Other kids leaned between and over them to get their ketchup and mustard, but no one spoke to them. My heart broke. They were different, and they knew it. I decided to sit with, befriend, and encourage them to risk approaching others. Over time, a few kids were able to overcome their fears, but others remained isolated and defeated by woundedness or impairments they didn't understand. I, the girl with dreams about running into burning buildings, was discovering that not all attempted rescues were successful.

In fifth grade, I joined the safety patrol to help other children cross the street as they walked to and from school. My corner assignment was farthest from the school, and I usually had to hurry the stragglers along all the way to the front doors to make it to my class before the bell rang. I was never even considered when time came to appoint a safety patrol lieutenant in sixth grade. Was I invisible? Misjudged? Was it because I was a girl? I had developed independent thinking, problem-solving and conflict-resolution skills, and a sense of personal responsibility while learning to survive in my parents' home. Didn't they notice that? This disappointment was my first encounter with feeling underestimated.

If opportunities to rescue people were limited at school, they still were plentiful at home. One scorching afternoon, my sisters' window fan got caught in the curtains, overheating the motor. The girls came running down the hall yelling, "Fire! Fire! Fire!" I filled a large pot with water in the kitchen sink, ran to the bedroom, unplugged the fan cord, and then doused the burning motor and curtains. I got a second pot and soaked the curtains and rug beneath them to be certain. I was still having burning-building nightmares occasionally—this would not help.

My grades were unremarkable no matter how hard I tried. I got As and Bs, especially in music and reading, but math and science didn't come easy, even at this level. I often struggled to understand and keep up as those subjects got more complex.

However, my sixth-grade teacher must have seen potential in me when he invited me to join a select group of students for field trips to the Hippodrome Theatre in Baltimore City to see travelogues filmed in exotic places around the world. One depicted nomadic tribes in southern Ethiopia whose women were adorned with metal rings around their necks that eventually distorted their proportions. They lived very primitively. My imagination was stimulated, and the images were permanently imprinted in my mind and heart. *These people need to know about Jesus.*

My responsibilities at home made extracurricular activities out of reach . Still, I discovered creative ways to circumvent the restraints of my current situation and build a social life. I would walk several miles to meet friends at the local lunch counter or diner to chat or go window-shopping at the strip mall whenever Mom remained home on the weekends. I never bought anything—I liked being one of the girls doing normal, preteen, girl things.

CHAPTER 5—THE GREAT JUNIOR HIGH SEWING CATASTROPHE

Advancement to junior high meant Home Economics, and I detested Home Economics. Not that I didn't appreciate the subjects being taught or learning how to roast a chicken or bake cookies. I did. I was terrified and intimidated because my mother hadn't taught me these basics, because she hadn't learned them herself. They were foreign to me—not boiling an egg—but other tasks, like sewing.

Students were required to make a piece of clothing from a pattern and wear it to school to get a final grade. I knew this was going to end badly! I was clueless about patterns, thread, fabric, sewing machines, fitting, hemming, you name it. In the 1960s, garment patterns were tissue thin, oddly shaped, with solid and dotted lines. They needed to be assembled with straight pins, inside out, upside down. It was all very mysterious and unsettling to me. I was drawn to the attractive rendering of the finished product on the cover of the pattern packet, but making that happen with what I was given seemed impossible.

I chose to make a simple blouse. The class was large, and the teacher assumed I could follow directions with minimal assistance, and all would be fine.

Well, it wasn't. I was reduced to tears as I slipped the ill-fitting blouse over my head in the girls' bathroom before class. After class, I made an excuse to leave early. Sneaking out a back door near the gym, I tossed the crumpled semblance of a short-sleeved blouse into a nearby trash can. I headed home alone, dejected, ashamed of my ignorance, failure, and inability to master this task.

Though Home Economics was my darkest moment, school had bright spots as well. In eighth grade, one teacher handed me an extra paper at midterm along with my report card. I was sure it was going to be negative, but it was a special merit award for outstanding character and performance in the classroom. She never knew how deeply her act of kindness affected me, nor how it positively impacted my sense of self-worth.

Not all my learning took place in a schoolroom during my junior high years.

I decided to read and soak up all the knowledge I could about the Bible and its message after my campfire commitment to give my all to Jesus at thirteen. Dad bought me *Nave's Topical Bible* from a student selling it house to house to earn tuition money for Bible college. I had to promise Dad I would use it since the book cost money he didn't have for such a thing. I still have my *Nave's* and routinely use it even though online access is freely available. *I'm keeping my promise, Dad.*

The impact of my campfire experience was also enriched by Elisabeth Elliot's book, *Through Gates of Splendor.*[1] She recounted the inspiring story of her husband, Jim, who was martyred, along with four friends, by a small group of isolated Waodani tribal warriors of Quito, Ecuador, in 1956. He had willingly given up his earthly life to demonstrate how they could gain access to eternal life through faith in Jesus Christ. My young heart embraced this extraordinary model of agapē love—sacrificially laying down one's life for another.

Uncle Dick and Aunt Margarette gave me *The Complete Works of Shakespeare* when I completed eighth grade. I read the whole volume that summer including all the sonnets. Learning was not a pastime—it was a lifeline.

The Miracle Worker movie came out in 1962. It is the story of how Annie Sullivan, a sight-impaired orphaned child committed to an insane asylum, graduated and dedicated herself to helping other disabled children in difficulty. She heard about the young Helen Keller who was left deaf, mute, and blind from a disease. Annie lovingly pursued Helen and finally broke through her dark silence with the awareness of how to communicate using sign language. This remarkable breakthrough was a testament to Annie's persistent, indefatigable devotion to Helen and her groundbreaking teaching methods, discovered through trial and error. They remained constant companions, teacher and student, kindred spirits until Annie passed away. Helen became an educated, accomplished advocate for people with disabilities, defying all accepted stereotypes about the deaf, mute, and blind. Annie became my heroine. I didn't know if they loved Jesus the way I did, but they sure lived as if they did.

My appetite to learn and grow was being met by many of the world's finest teachers! I could not know as a young teen about the string of losses that would mark the years ahead of me, but I was already growing intimate with the teachers and storytellers who would see me through those losses.

Carol was a good friend in junior high school. She was one of a group of girls who seemed to accept and include me. They were more streetwise and boy crazy than I was, but I enjoyed doing things with them. Carol was a standout in the group: tall and lanky, with a deep voice like mine, and privately, a deep thinker. She was pragmatic and quiet and possessed an air of confidence.

"Mom, can you drive me to Carol's house? She invited me over," I asked on a fateful day.

"Yes, I'm going in that direction," Mom answered unexpectedly, and off we went.

As I got out of the car, Mom said, "Wait, I want to tell you something. I have met another man I like very much. Hank. When I am not home, I am usually with him. I need to tell you this so that in an emergency you can get in touch with me. Here is his phone number. Don't tell your father."

I stood alone on the sidewalk in front of Carol's house, blindsided by a tornado. I was fourteen.

"God! Enough!" I screamed after she drove away. *I want out. Are you listening to me? No more.*

I needed a plan. Be gone as much as possible until tenth grade starts in September: junior helper at Sunday school and summer Bible school, one week at Overcomers camp, and two weeks at Bonnie's house in New Jersey. We were kindred spirits. Invite friends and cousins to our pool. Take care of Jessie and Cassie. Keep reading. Immerse myself in studying the Bible and memorizing verses.

God, help my sisters and me survive this relentless nightmare.

While I was at summer camp, Mom told Dad her secret, then asked him to leave and invited Hank to move in. But several months later, Mom discovered she had cancerous lesions in her mouth. Frightened, she made Hank move out and asked Dad to move back in, which he did. He promised to change, and she promised never to see Hank again.

Months after the surgery to remove the cancer, with the crisis seemingly fading from memory, Mom became restless again. Moody. Unpleasant. Gradually she made excuses about needing to work longer or visit friends. Time at home with us subtly decreased.

God, I hate being yanked around. I hate Mom's lying. What are you doing? Adultery. Cancer. Empty promises. What do you expect from me? Why can't they change? Will this pain ever end?

I would tell myself, *Don't think about that. God knows everything. He's in charge.* And I would recall the wisdom from my Bible: "Trust in the Lord with all your heart and lean not on your own understanding; in all your ways submit to him, and he will make your paths straight" (Prov. 3:5–6).

I'm trusting, leaning, acknowledging, waiting for you to straighten my path. When, Lord? How much longer?

One afternoon the kitchen phone rang. "Hello," I said.

"Mary?" the caller responded.

I froze in place. I knew it was Hank. The phone call ended abruptly. I was livid, overcome by a sense of betrayal. She'd been lying to me, to Dad, to everyone, again and again. I detested lying. It made me nauseated.

What would happen if Dad had to leave again? He represented stability and security despite all his other relational inadequacies. Surely he would leave if he knew the affair had resumed. What about Jessie and Cassie? They are still so young. What would divorce mean for all of us?

I couldn't identify anyone to confide in as a multitude of questions swirled around my head. My Bible told me, "Be still, and know that I am God" (Ps. 46:10).

Yes, God, I know you're God, but I don't know how to be still. And I hate feeling helpless. Lord, send your warrior angels and calm my fears. I can't do this alone.

Mom remained married to Dad while having an ongoing affair with Hank. I held this secret in painful silence for ten dreadful years. I was hopelessly trapped in her charade, attempting to protect myself and my sisters at Dad's expense, although I was not responsible for his avoidance and denial. I wasn't responsible for any of this, yet I was destined to carry heavy burdens not meant for a child, struggling daily to make sense out of the senseless. Food was a constant consoling companion, yet it provided none of the happiness and joy I longed for. Deep wounds, hidden sorrows—no end in sight—these all left permanent scars still visible, though faded, today.

CHAPTER 6—HIGH SCHOOL HIGHS AND LOWS

In 1965, Baltimore County Board of Education, in all its learned wisdom, drew new high school boundary lines at my street. Friends north and east of that line went to Milford Mill High School. I went to Woodlawn.

I didn't know one person, teen, or adult when the school bus dropped me off at Woodlawn on the first day of school. Schedule in hand, I found my first class. Biology. I took my assigned seat in the first row next to the window and waited to see who would join me. At the last second as the bell stopped ringing, a bubbly, ponytailed blonde with a big smile quickly slid into the empty chair next to me after high-fiving all the kids in the front row.

"Hi, my name is Joni," she whispered. "What's yours?"

"Diana," I replied quietly. "Glad to meet you."

Before we all rushed out when the next bell rang, I said, "Joni, I'm new here, I don't know anybody."

"Don't worry about that," she said. "I know everybody. Stick with me. You'll be fine."

I did. I was. God had answered my prayers.

Joni and I shared many classes and teachers, which added to the fun and camaraderie of our friendship. Joni introduced me to Young Life, a Christian organization that invited high schoolers to get to know Jesus and follow him. I had found a mission outpost among new friends who were in pursuit of spiritual things but had no idea what they were yet.

"Hey, kids, sign up for a 'Weekend to Remember' at Natural Bridge, Virginia. We'll travel to the hotel on a charter bus and together will have lots of fun, food, and fellowship. It will be the best weekend of your life," Chuck Reinhold, our club leader, announced one Wednesday night.

I rushed home. "Dad, I'm so excited about Woodlawn's Young Life Club. They do funny skits, sing Scripture songs, and talk about Jesus. Chuck says, 'It's a sin to bore a kid with the gospel.' He makes it come alive, and all my friends seem interested in knowing more. Can I go with them this weekend to Virginia, please? It's only one hundred dollars for the bus, hotel, food, and activities from Friday evening through Sunday evening? Please! Please!"

I was devastated by his response: "I can't afford it. I'm sorry."

I could have asked for a scholarship but didn't know it then. Years later, I became a Young Life Committee Chairman in my county and made certain that any club kid who wanted to go to a weekend retreat or summer camp would not miss out for lack of funds.

I cried all weekend, alone in my room. Between sobs, I murmured prayers for each person on that trip. "Touch their hearts with your grace and unfailing love, Lord. Holy Spirit, compel them to understand the hopelessness of their sin, their desperate need of a Savior. May they receive the free gift of forgiveness and eternal life that you paid for by dying on a cross for their sin."

At school Monday morning, I heard story after story of decisions to accept Christ as Lord and Savior. People couldn't stop sharing what they heard and experienced. Joni particularly sought me out: "Di, I want to know more about all of this. Can you come to my house this week so we can talk?"

What happened that weekend—the many spiritual new births, that invitation from Joni to come to her house, and the way God answered the prayers of a disappointed teenage girl—were seismic earthquakes in my life.

♫

Music was my thing. Before I could talk or walk, I was singing and making music at home, church, school, anywhere, everywhere, and with anyone who could stay on key. I routinely squeezed the maximum number of music classes into my academic schedule and found my place to belong. Woodlawn was no exception. Mr. Blackwell, my high school choir director, recognized my potential and nurtured it for three years, giving me many opportunities to blossom, perform, improve, and share this God-given talent.

I found many friends in choir, madrigal, and girls chorus. How we enjoyed making beautiful sounds together as we mastered challenging musical scores in four-part harmony! Mr. Blackwell introduced us to challenging classical religious and secular music and broadened our knowledge and interest in great music.

I had made many friends by my sixteenth birthday with choir, Joni's introductions, and Young Life. I pushed and pushed until my parents agreed I could have a sleepover party. I invited my girlfriends for food, fun, and games, and they all came and came—thirty or more! Sleeping bags, pillows, guitars, you name it, they brought it. I hadn't anticipated how all these people were going to fit into our tiny house. What a hoot!

They slept under the dining room table, under the kitchen table, up the hallway, under the piano bench. The toilet flushed all night, and no one got much sleep for the singing, giggling, and chatting. It was wonderful! In the morning, all belongings were packed up, and laughter still filled the house and driveway as the girls left. People still talk about it today and laugh. What was I thinking?

I continued to struggle with gaining and losing weight. Attending dances was taboo in my denomination. No prom. But I made the best of what I had and enjoyed what socializing was available to me. Overall, high school was a positive experience.

$$\mathscr{D}$$

Dad assumed and expected I would go to college but provided no practical help in how to make that happen. Neither he nor Mom had any personal experience with higher education and were not inclined to help with my planning or seeking counsel.

At age five, I had declared I wanted to be a doctor after being inspired by our old-fashioned family doctor who relieved my excruciating pain from an acute ear infection. I wanted to do that for others. However, music and history were my forté and dominated my course selections in high school. I was weak in math and science—my grades in chemistry, algebra, and geometry were average and unremarkable, and I had avoided trigonometry altogether. Though I did my best to excel despite the constant distractions at home, the die was cast concerning my academic future. Unfortunately, I didn't know it yet.

CHAPTER 7-CAPE MAY

In May 1967, one week after graduation from Woodlawn High School, I headed off to Cape May, New Jersey, in my powder-blue Ford Fairlane for my first job. I worked in the canteen of the Christian Admiral Hotel as a short-order cook, manager, and ice-cream-float maker extraordinaire.[1] From my perch on the manager's stool, I could enjoy the Atlantic Ocean's foamy breakers as they rhythmically rose and crashed over the rocky barrier walls across the street, at the tip of Jersey's peninsula. The smell of salt air, the constancy of sea breeze, and working with a few close friends at the shore promised to make a memorable summer before we all dispersed for college and the dreams we were pursuing.

Early in June, Shelton College caught my attention.[2] It was located on the Christian Admiral campus. I discovered I could earn a bachelor's degree in Biblical Studies, a precursor to foreign missions or other types of full-time Christian work. Many Overcomers friends were enrolled for fall semester. I had no money for tuition, but the Admissions Office encouraged me to apply for several scholarships and loans. They were confident that if God wanted me there, finances could be worked out. Even though I had applied and been accepted at the University of Maryland Baltimore County (UMBC) to pursue a BA in PreMed, there was still time to apply to Shelton College for entry-level coursework leading to a BA in Bible, then eventually an MA in Theology.

Meanwhile I was thriving under my newfound independence. The environment at Cape May and the Christian Admiral Hotel was ideal for me. I was outgoing, loved to laugh, and loved to make new friends. One of those new friends worked as a waitress in the large, formal dining room at the hotel. Sadly, I no longer remember her name; nevertheless, she played an important part in my life.

August, which arrived too quickly, found me treasuring this sacred time between exuberant youth and conscientious adulthood. I was loving life and dreaming big dreams.

PART 3

CHAPTER 8–I DON'T REMEMBER HER NAME

One morning before I clocked in at the canteen, I walked by the rooming house where one of my new friends lived. It was one of several such buildings on the hotel's spacious campus: A large, five-story Victorian with lots of gingerbread decoration along the roof edges. A plaque over the entrance declared it to be The Morning Star. *How poetic and biblical!*

I looked up and saw my friend on the roof, inching along a thin edge of curled up asphalt tiles outside her fourth-floor corner window. She had a hammer in her hand and was trying to pry off an old window screen to gain easier access to an extended section of the roof. There, she could comfortably stretch out on her beach towel and soak in the sun's morning rays before setting off to wait tables.

"If that screen comes loose, you'll—" I never got to finish my sentence.

Suddenly the screen flew off. My brain recorded the fall in slow motion as I ran toward her. To catch her. To break her fall.

She fell backward, hitting her head violently on an adjacent building's roof, and was then thrust forward in the opposite direction, hitting the first building with her chest. Then she was again thrust backward, bouncing hard against the ground right in front of me.

Could she still be alive? Yes. But her shallow breathing was labored and crackly. She was nonresponsive. Her eyes were rolling in her head, and blood was beginning to fill her mouth and drip down her chin. She had sustained three life-threatening traumas to her body in rapid succession.

I screamed, "Somebody call an ambulance! Help! Help! HELP! Somebody call an ambulance!" not knowing if anyone heard me. I didn't want to leave my friend's side. I spoke to her, trying to detect a response. I pleaded with God to spare her life.

The scream of an ambulance siren grew louder and louder. "Hurry, hurry, hurry," I murmured, as I touched her hand and gently stroked her face. In hushed tones, I prayed Psalm 23 over her: "Even though I walk through the darkest valley, I will fear no evil, for you are with me; your rod and your staff, they comfort me … Surely your goodness and love will follow me all the days of my life, and I will dwell in the house of the Lord forever." I envisioned the poster I loved from the old church hall, the Good Shepherd rescuing his endangered lamb.

The paramedics swiftly put her on a stretcher, slid her into the back of the vehicle, and sped off to the nearest hospital, siren blaring again. A stranger, an older woman, approached and asked if I would like a ride to the emergency room. I quietly answered, "Yes. Please."

When I arrived, I sat in a hallway chair by myself, waiting for news from someone, anyone. Praying silently. Too numb for tears. The tragic scene kept replaying in my mind. What could I have done differently? Why couldn't I run fast enough to catch her, to cushion her fall, to minimize her injuries? Then I recognized if I had reached her before she hit the ground, I would have been severely injured also. So many haunting, unanswerable questions.

Mr. Murphy, the Christian Admiral Hotel director, finally arrived and found me in the hallway. "She's gone," he said. "There was nothing they could do to save her. The police would like to talk to you. Can you do that now?"

"Yes," I replied.

The next day, I spoke to her grieving parents, more people from the hotel management, and numerous others. I don't remember who they all were. By late afternoon, I had repacked my car with the remaining fragments of my aborted senior summer at the ocean and set out on the three-hour drive to Baltimore, numb and confused.

This senseless tragedy reignited childhood nightmares of running into burning buildings. But this was no longer a dream—it was real. And I was helpless to rescue her.

"Oh God," I cried out, "why didn't you stretch out your powerful arm and rescue this one precious lamb? I couldn't rescue her, but *you* could have!"

I needed to make sense out of this sudden, tragic death but found none. The cascade of apparent contradictions assaulted what I knew about God and what I assumed I knew about myself. These questions would torment me until I found answers.

Lord, I feel helpless. I know you are here beside me as I drive home. Please, speak to me.

Something intangible, yet permanent, happened that day. I gained a sobering sense of my own mortality. At the same time, the assurance of promised immortality comforted and motivated me as God's indwelling Spirit brought Psalm 90:12 to my mind: "Teach us to number our days, that we may gain a heart of wisdom."

Thank you, Lord, for this answer. I will spend the rest of my days seeking to know and love you more.

CHAPTER 9—SHOCK TRAUMA

I barely recall packing up and leaving Cape May. By the time I got home, I desperately needed to be with someone, to stop replaying the deadly fall scene in my mind, and to reconnect with a simple, safe semblance of life going on as anticipated. I sought out Sharon, a high school choir friend, who lived a few miles from my neighborhood.

I arrived unannounced and was relieved to find her. She hadn't left for college yet. She greeted me at the screen door and said, "Come in and have a soda. I have bad news to give you."

Before any words could form in my mind about my own bad news, Sharon told me that Joni was in Shock Trauma at the University of Maryland Medical Center in Baltimore City.

"What happened? How long has she been there? Have you seen her? Can I get in to see her? Please tell me more."

Sharon had only heard that Joni had a bad accident several weeks ago, and they didn't know whether she would live or not.

I was stunned. Two days ago, one new friend died, and now my best friend was fighting to live. How could this be?

I thanked Sharon and immediately drove downtown to the hospital. I knew how to get there but had never gone inside.

I went through the right motions. Parked the car. Found the main entrance. Went to the front desk. Asked for patient information. "Has my friend been admitted here? What floor? What room? Can I go up and visit now?"

The fifth-floor elevators opened onto a specialized intensive care unit filled with people in critical condition surrounded by trauma doctors and nurses who constantly monitored each patient.

I found Joni. Motionless. Lying on a Stryker frame, a special bed that rotated her body from face up to face down to prevent bed sores. Her hair was matted. A wide swath had been shaved off from ear to ear to position and affix metal tongs embedded on either side of her skull to keep her broken vertebra in traction. This protected them from further injury and gave her spine space to deal with swelling and inflammation. She was covered by a white sheet up to her shoulders. Tubes all around, machines humming quietly, urine bag dangling from the bed frame.

"Hi, Jon," I quietly said in her ear.

"Hi, Di," she faintly replied. "Would you scratch my nose please? I can't reach it."

During the previous three weeks, she had survived the initial phase of shock and a three-hour emergency surgery that inserted a metal plate with each end screwed into the broken vertebrae to stabilize the area, thus taking pressure off the spinal cord. Being an excellent athlete in good physical condition added to Joni's odds of living versus dying.

Hospitals are a world unto themselves. When a loved one is admitted to intensive care, you instantly become part of this surreal world of an elite group: ordinary folks randomly selected for a special type of suffering and pain, known only to those who have experienced it. I discovered, years later, that the University of Maryland Medical Center had opened its Shock Trauma unit, the first one in the United States, not long before Joni's accident. It kept severely injured patients alive long enough for the body to survive the ravages of shock and to increase their chances of surviving life-threatening injuries.

Joni's stay in Shock Trauma began when she took a deep dive off a wooden raft at a Chesapeake Bay beach and forcefully struck her forehead on the sandy bottom, breaking the fourth and fifth vertebra in her neck, causing a transverse injury to her spinal cord. If her sister Kathy hadn't been in the water close enough to notice Joni's limp body floating face down, she would have drowned. Kathy pulled Joni's head to the surface as she gasped for breath— her legs, arms, and hands were permanently paralyzed. My friend was seventeen.

By the time I found her in Shock Trauma, it was clear Joni was going to survive. But could she or would she fight this thing? How deep were her internal resources to overcome a lifetime of overwhelming obstacles? Her life was irreversibly interrupted by a split-second decision. Her earthly house, her body, had figuratively burned to the ground. Yet what could I possibly do to help? I didn't know how to respond to a person facing a lifetime in a wheelchair.

Would I run away from the ruins of Joni's altered life or would I run toward the ruins, knowingly altering my own life, because she was my friend and I loved her? Would I, could I, do what my childhood heroine Annie Sullivan had done for Helen Keller in *The Miracle Worker*?

CHAPTER 10-RIGHT TIME, RIGHT PLACE, RIGHT REASON

As I wrestled with how to help my friend, Jesus's words came to mind: "Love your neighbor as yourself" (Matt. 22:39). In my eighteen years, I had heard or read that verse hundreds of times. But now, I was compelled to understand more fully what it meant, for this time and this situation.

When I defined *neighbors*, I'd always pictured people who lived on my street. Loving them meant being thoughtful toward them—picking up occasional trash on their lawns, catching Muffin, a terrier, when he got out of his fenced-in yard, and things like that.

I also considered the kids at school as neighbors. I was watchful over the lonely ones who sat by themselves during lunchtime, who were bullied on the playground, or who were always chosen last for the tag team during recess. Yes, I was confident that being sensitive and inclusive of classmates also qualified as loving my neighbor.

But Joni's crisis was forcing me to recognize a far more serious form of loving my neighbor—loving in adversity. I recalled a Bible verse I had memorized long ago: "A friend loves at all times, and a brother is born for a time of adversity" (Prov. 17:17). All times? In adversity? That's more complicated than my previous understanding of loving my neighbor.

And me of all people? My past was strewn with brokenness. Not like Joni's paralysis, but deep and overwhelming, nonetheless. What could I offer in the face of the external and internal struggles I was already dealing with?

It came to me simply, gently. I could love Joni by being present. I could share my heart, my struggles, my pain. I could share spiritual insights learned through knock-down, drag-out battles with my own demons. I was still in the midst of many struggles, but I had survived many as well, and I could help Joni drink deeply from the reservoir of God's mercy and love as I had learned to do. We could plumb the mysteries of such things together as we fought through the challenges of each new day. We could live out the wisdom in Ecclesiastes 4:9–10.

> Two are better than one,
> because they have a good return for their labor:
> If either of them falls down,
> one can help the other up.

I could stay in Baltimore. I could commit myself to joining Joni on her long journey back to a life worth living. I intuitively knew I was in the right place, at the right time, for a purpose that was far greater than myself. Eighteen years of lessons learned prepared me for this moment of decision and all that was to come from it.

As I consciously made that decision to love Joni with my presence, a reassuring sense of peacefulness descended on my mind and heart.

Now that I had a compelling reason to stay in Baltimore, I released my dream to attend Shelton College and quickly finalized my full-time enrollment as a freshman at UMBC. I paid the tuition, adjusted my academic schedule where possible, and reordered my daily life to be available for Joni.

I had been attending the school of adversity for the first eighteen years of my life. Now was the time and place to apply all I had learned, for the right reason.

CHAPTER 11—THE COLLEGE KID

UMBC, here I come. This commuter-only University of Maryland campus on the west side of Baltimore launched in 1966. It started small but already had a premed track in its second year of operation. I still dreamed of becoming a doctor and was eager to meet the challenges in front of me.

Most of my peers' parents had never attended college. Although they couldn't help us navigate the arduous web of registration requirements or select and schedule classes, we all persisted. That first day of class was the culmination of my father's goal of sending the first of his three daughters to college and my goal of healing the sick of the world.

The first semester of general courses included a premed favorite, Biology 101, and another more formidable goal, Inorganic Chemistry 101. I zigzagged through beltway rush hour traffic, competed for a convenient parking space close to the first class, and got busy making new friends.

One day, a flashy poster on the theater/lecture hall door caught my attention. It advertised auditions for the 1967 freshman semester theater production of *Bus Stop*. I went to tryouts (remembering all the fun I had under Aunt Blanche's dramatic tutelage) and got the part of Gracie, the short-order cook. I found a sense of belonging there. Fall semester sped by acting on stage or at play practice, sitting in lecture halls, driving to and from visiting Joni, and studying at home until midnight while minding my sisters.

I had grouped my classes early in the morning or late in the afternoon. This allowed me to visit Joni at the hospital during the day. In October, Joni transferred to Greendale, a local rehabilitation hospital, where she remained for approximately one year. I became a part-time volunteer Candy Striper at Greendale. The place resembled a warehouse for useless and hopeless inmates. Those were the early days of figuring out what to do with people who survived catastrophic injuries and were often abandoned or marginalized by family and friends.

I struggled through inorganic chemistry and became concerned as the day approached to see my first-semester grades. The long envelope with a colorful UMBC return address label finally arrived around noon on a frosty day in January 1968. It never reached the mailbox. I grabbed a bundle of mail from the postman's hand and eagerly fingered through the fliers, magazines, and letters looking for the anticipated envelope, the coveted (or dreaded) prize.

Standing outside in the cold, I deciphered a B in biology. Good. Then, inorganic chemistry, a foundational premed course. I was hoping for a C, at worst a D. I had joined a study group and poured over lecture notes and heavy textbooks all semester.

It was an F. I went into shock. I was burnt toast. My efforts had been valiant, but I had failed miserably. The reality that math and science were not my strengths had caught up with me. I was ill-informed about possible resources or remedial courses that might have made a difference. I could see no other outcome: my goal of becoming a missionary doctor vanished. I descended into depression. *Help me Jesus. This can't be the end of my dream to become a doctor.*

I slept restlessly, tossing and turning for weeks. And as I did, these words kept scrolling through my subconscious mind: "For I know the plans I have for you," declares the Lord, "plans to prosper you and not to harm you, plans to give you hope and a future" (Jer. 29:11). I kept repeating God's promises. *Hope and a future. Hope and a future. He's been so faithful for so long. He won't abandon me now. God's got plans for me. He promised. He keeps his promises.*

And finally: *Pick yourself up off the floor, girl. Help is on the way.*

While I was wallowing, I had bright moments of remembering the pure enjoyment of acting and theater that had nurtured new friendships for me that fall. One dream may have died, but now, at the persistent lobbying by the department head, I switched majors from premed to speech and theater and secondary education. Was I impetuously squandering my academic years at UMBC in the theater department? All I knew was that I loved to act and direct. And my fellow thespians said I had good comic timing. Innate aptitudes for creativity, resourcefulness, and enthusiasm were nurtured and expanded. In years to come, the producing, directing, stage managing, and acting skills proved surprisingly useful in many contexts.

It was great to be majoring in a subject I was good at! Yet I continued to struggle with letting go of my unrealistic plans to become a medical doctor. I still had conversations with God that sounded a lot like this:

Why, God? Why did you make me this way? Why didn't you give me math and science genes? Why didn't you make me smarter? I had a good plan like Jim Elliot and Annie Sullivan. What about all of that? What about that campfire commitment? Here I am, Lord, send me!

I can make people laugh. So what? How's that going to help those women in the remote villages of Ethiopia who need medical care?

My family is poor. My father is sacrificially funding my college education so I can transcend the circumstantial boundaries he faced. This is his dream, God, and what are you doing with it? What am I truly able to do with it?

I identified with the lamb in the poster again, frantically clinging to the jagged cliff edge, desperately hoping to be rescued. Rapidly slipping into depression, I would cry out, "Jesus, I'm over here. Over here. Help. Help. Please help me now. Before all is lost."

God had a plan. He has always had a perfect plan for me, but I didn't know it yet.

CHAPTER 12—CALIFORNIA, HERE WE COME

As the end of 1968 approached, it became painfully obvious that the rehab facility was a dead end for Joni. She had spent many months on a Stryker frame, still unable to sit upright in a chair. She developed several bed sores and bladder infections. Her dad, John Eareckson, wasted no time in having Joni transferred to Rancho Los Amigos National Rehabilitation Center in Downey, California. Joni's sister, Jay, offered to move to California to be Joni's family representative and advocate while Joni received the best physical and occupational therapy available in the United States.

Jay needed to drive cross-country with household basics and move into a rented apartment until Joni gained strength and mobility and could return home to Maryland. That meant driving three thousand miles on the southern route from Baltimore to Los Angeles in the family station wagon in January. Dickie and Jackie, Joni's close high school friends, volunteered for the three-day, lightning-speed road trip. A few days after reaching Los Angeles, they would fly home to resume college and work.

I decided to seize this opportunity, postpone my spring classes, take the necessary fifteen credits later and volunteer to join the driving team. I would remain in California with Jay for two months to learn and practice all the details of how to physically care for Joni's needs: changing catheters, doing range-of-motion exercises, and more.

What a trip! We only stopped for gas and food. Two slept while two drove. We stayed overnight at the Bright Angel Lodge inside Grand Canyon Park to give the drivers and the station wagon a good night's rest. A stationary blanket of dense fog shrouded our view as we peered over the railing outside the hotel door at one of the wonders of the world. Oh, well. I could say I'd been there.

The cross-country trip and the time spent in California expanded my horizons. I'd never traveled west of the Appalachian Mountains or ever known a person living with quadriplegia before Joni. I had a lot to process mentally as I flew home (my first airplane ride) two months later. Mom helped me find a job at Sinai Hospital, which I kept until the fall semester at UMBC began in September 1968.

Rancho discharged Joni in April 1969, when the goals and limits of her physical and occupational therapy were reached: sitting upright in a wheelchair for extended periods of time, feeding herself with a spork stuck in her arm brace, turning pages with limp fingers dangling from wrist braces, and writing and drawing with a pencil or brush in her mouth. The long-term prognosis was confirmed—the paralysis in her arms, hands, and legs was permanent.

Joni and Jay returned to the Eareckson home in Woodlawn. The dining room with its large fireplace, big windows, and ground-level access became her new residence.

Mr. Eareckson was a successful retired businessman and a loving, generous dad. Lindy, Joni's mom, made the house a warm and loving home, but the trauma of Joni's accident occasionally overcame her resilience. Occasionally, she dipped in and out of exhaustion and depression.

Simultaneously, my distress at home sank to new depths.

CHAPTER 13—A FATHER'S BETRAYAL

My sophomore semester (September 1969) began with a full load of theater and education courses. Jay and I had figured out how to enable Joni to take a public speaking class with me at UMBC. It took a lot of effort but was great fun.

I still lived at home but spent non-class time with Joni in Woodlawn when I wasn't studying or chauffeuring my sisters to and from their after-school activities. Dad was rarely home at night before I went to bed, but after he built the piano workroom onto the back of the house, he spent more and more evenings there.

One evening, Mom was out as usual. Dad unexpectedly engaged me in conversation while I was getting dinner in the kitchen.

"I know you haven't had much experience with dating," he began. "You're older now and boys will begin to ask you out on dates. You need to be careful. Sometimes boys try to take advantage of young girls like you. They might try to do things to you."

He walked over to where I was standing, backed me up against the wall, and began to kiss me on the neck. I became rigid, unable to move or speak. I was in shock, frightened, repulsed, and screaming inside with panic and disbelief. As my flight impulse kicked in, I slowly nudged him away without a word and retreated to my bedroom, locking the door behind me. Eventually he went back to his workbench, which was on the other side of my bedroom window. I lay awake in the night, tears streaming down my face, fearing he might come to my door.

The next morning, I drove to UMBC, parked on an empty lot, and prayed. "God, is this part of your plan for me? How could it be?"

However absent and unavailable Dad was, his presence was the anchor holding things in place, even if tentatively. His betrayal convinced me I needed to leave home. But where would I go? Who should I talk to?

I was hesitant to tell anyone what happened. Dad had already endured decades of his own unspoken traumas—no wonder he momentarily lost his mind, or so I told myself. I called our family doctor. He offered no help or advice, only "Don't tell your mother." I guess he feared she would finally kill Dad this time.

No help there. No protection. I was reminded of Psalm 32:7: "You are my hiding place; you will protect me from trouble and surround me with songs of deliverance." *Help me Jesus*, I prayed.

I went to my classes, then over to Joni's house. She sensed my distress. At her urging, I recounted what had happened the previous night. We talked for a long time. I don't remember what was said, but I do remember what we decided. I needed to move out of my father's house, and she needed more focused attention than her family could give her at the time. I would leave my home in Lochearn and move into Joni's home in Woodlawn.

I went home that evening while Dad was out working and briefly told my mother what Dad had done. I packed my suitcase and calmly informed her I would be moving into Joni's house and not moving back home. I didn't even say goodbye to my sisters. I never talked to Mom or Dad again about the night Dad inappropriately touched me. It was too painful. God would forgive him, and I would forgive him with God's help. We acted as if it never happened, and life went on as usual, but it didn't. It seemed like the right time for me to put this latest betrayal, along with all the other betrayals, in the rear-view mirror and get on with life.

CHAPTER 14 — TURNING POINT

I returned to Joni's house one afternoon after my classes to find her staring out the window, daydreaming. Our Woodlawn yearbook lay open on a music stand positioned between her motionless legs. I didn't interrupt, I silently observed. She lingered there for an hour or more, occasionally turning pages with paralyzed fingers supported by a leather wrist brace.

Finally, I spoke. "Don't lose the life you've been given by holding on to the life you've lost."

Joni refused to make eye contact. I drew closer, grabbed her face between my hands, and looked into her eyes. "You've got to stop doing this." She shut her eyes to shut me out. I grabbed both shoulders firmly and got closer in her face. "Come back to the life you have. See what God will do. This is not the end; it's a new beginning. Run with it, Jon, don't give up."

Thankfully, few days were like that. Typically, she pursued fun with gusto.

"I love to sing at Union Station downtown. Those vaulted ceilings make great acoustics. Let's go!" Joni exclaimed. Craig, Chuck, Joni, and I (tenor, base, soprano, and alto) piled into the car and headed downtown. It was 10:30 p.m.

"Amazing grace, how sweet the sound, that saved a wretch like me. I once was lost but now am found, was blind but now I see."[1] We sang in perfect acapella harmony.

Spirits soared as our praise and worship continued until a janitor with an enormous broom spotted us.

"Hey, you. Yes, you, girlie. Put that wheelchair back where you got it. It's midnight, and you need to get out of here or I'll call the cops!"

We burst into raucous laughter unable to contain the humor and irony of the moment.

"I mean it," insisted the janitor. "Get up! Put that chair back. Now!"

Barely able to speak, gasping for breath, I responded, "The chair is hers!" I picked up Joni's arms and let them drop. I lifted one leg and let it drop. The guys were bent over, exhausted from laughter and no help at all.

"Give me that chair! Get out of here!"

I grabbed Joni from behind, folded her arms in front of her waist, and lifted her off the seat cushion several inches. "See? She's paralyzed. She can't walk. This chair is hers."

Finally. Embarrassed and confused, the janitor turned and walked away.

We threw Joni in the car, the chair in the trunk and sped away. We were buoyant. It was reassuring to fool the janitor so convincingly. Joni was still Joni, sitting or walking. Impressions are defined by point of view or subjective perception, and hers were changing as she got more comfortable with her new state of being.

As summer changed to fall, the Eareckson home became a vibrant community center on any given day or night, regularly packed with drop-in friends eager to visit Joni and grab a seat on a growing movement of young adults pursuing God and seeking answers to life's most puzzling dilemmas. Joni's irresistible personality and the staggering marathon she unwillingly entered, magnetically engaged all who knew her. Boisterous singing and laughter often filled the room. Fiercely competitive Monopoly games unfolded as we crowded together around the oversized fireplace her father had built in the spacious dining room, now Joni's bedroom and center of gravity.

At other times, hushed voices read Scripture, offered earnest prayers, expressed heartfelt confessions, and made lifelong commitments. They could scarcely be heard over the crackling flames of the fire that cast an eerie glow of kneeling shadows across the room, up the walls, and onto the ceiling. We knew life-changing transformations were happening among and in us. God's presence was palpable.

CHAPTER 15—ESTABLISHING ROUTINES AND FINDING ANSWERS

Jay, Joni, and I eventually moved out of the Woodlawn home into horse country near Sykesville. Joni's father had purchased a large tract of land years ago adjacent to the Patapsco State Park with endless trails and fields for horseback riding and a local rodeo he operated for a few years.

It had a big, red barn for their horses and hay, a remodeled sharecropper's house, and a manor house with outbuildings. Mr. Eareckson built a dorm for weekend cowboys and a show ring for the rodeo. As his three oldest daughters grew up, then married, he built each a rustic home on sections of the property, built corrals for their horses, and fenced off hayfields for harvesting.

Jay's house expanded when he added a large room with fireplace and picture windows for Joni to panoramically see the familiar horses, barn, and hay fields surrounding her. She read, studied, and painted at a long dining room table where friends often gathered to eat, talk, sing, and pray.

A functional daily rhythm evolved around Joni's needs. For her wake-up routine, we made sure she drank lots of water while going through thirty minutes of passive range of motion exercises for her arms and legs, then we administered a bed bath. Next, we put on the long canvas corset with metal stays that supported her diaphragm so she could inhale and exhale while sitting in her wheelchair. Then we'd turn her this way and that to put on support stockings and jeans. To get Joni out of bed, two people would sit her up, one grabbing her around the rib cage from behind and the other getting under both legs, and then one-two-three lifting her into a chair next to the bed.

Next: brush teeth, wash hair, blow nose, dry and style hair, and put bra, top, and maybe makeup on if going to an appointment.

Now we were ready to wheel her to the dining room table for breakfast. Jay fixed breakfast. I helped feed Joni and set her up for the morning with her art easel, music stand, paper, brushes, paint, books, calendar, and telephone. Then I drove the thirty-minute commute to UMBC for my day classes.

When I returned late in the afternoon, Joni and I shared our daytime happenings. We read the Bible and many other books together, enthusiastically discussing insights we gleaned from each chapter.

Joni's morning routine reversed at bedtime. We lifted her into bed, turned her on her side, stuffed various pillows in the right places, and placed her arms just so. My foldout sofa bed was right next to Joni's bed. I could raise or lower her's with a manual handle. We talked for a while and usually prayed together before drifting off to sleep. We occasionally challenged each other with who could recite the most Bible verses, verbatim, from memory. She would wake me up halfway through the night to turn her from one side to the other. This was essential to prevent bed sores. I quickly learned how to go right back to sleep.

At one point, inspired by a few acting and psychology courses, I got the idea to use role-play to iron out wrinkles in our routine. Jay and I sat Joni on the living room sofa, crossed her legs, and positioned one arm on the back cushion. We were surprised by how normal she appeared, as if she could stand and walk across the room. We took turns sitting in her wheelchair.

"Can you get me a drink of water, please?" Jay said, playing Joni's part. "Can't you wait a few minutes?" Joni said, playing the caregiver part. As we mimicked how this usually played out, we gained new insights into how caregivers and those requesting care feel, respond, and make assumptions about others. I took quiet delight in knowing my frivolous acting classes had provided such a practical application.

For two years as I did my commute to UMBC, fighting rush hour traffic in both directions, this basic daily routine continued at Jay's home. I still remember two terrifying experiences from my commute. One morning, I almost got squeezed between two converging eighteen-wheelers that never saw my little Ford Maverick. I slammed on the brakes, and the trucks continued as if nothing had happened. I was still shaking from the trauma when I parked near the lecture hall.

One hazardous winter morning during a blinding blizzard, I left the farm for an 8:00 a.m. class. I miraculously reached campus, crested Hilltop Road, hit the brakes, and slid down the steep incline, fully expecting to plow into a panel truck stuck at the bottom of the hill. I braced myself for impact and shouted out the quickest prayer I ever uttered, "Help!" My car stopped two inches from the truck's bumper. I envisioned an armored angel with shield up and sword raised commanding the car to stop. The truck driver, who looked like a polar bear walking on hind legs, approached my window.

"You've got powerful angels, young lady," he said. I agreed.

Despite my grueling schedule, I still had energy and a great hunger to learn more. I had accumulated a pocketful of spiritual golden nuggets during the previous twenty years which I pulled out and used as needed to survive each crisis and to keep moving forward. I believed that "in all things God works for the good of those who love him, who have been called according to his purpose" (Rom. 8:28), but I still struggled to accept as good all the mayhem and painful emotions I had endured. I had lots of unanswered questions. "Why?" questions were the most complicated.

Although I had good friends, girls and guys, and extended family that loved and affirmed me, I still struggled with self-esteem, unable to fully accept my mediocre, genetic hard-wiring. I didn't excel at anything, and I desperately wanted to. Yo-yo weight gain and loss left me self-conscious, plump, and left out of adolescent and young adult social scenes like dancing, parties, and dating. I wasn't content with the parents God selected for me with their limitations and emotional baggage. Growing up poor narrowed many options that friends effortlessly enjoyed, like taking family vacations, being given the things they needed and wanted, etc.

God's big picture for me was still elusive. I purposed to pursue him more intensely until I discovered more answers to my questions, more contentment in his purposes, and more joy along the journey ahead of me.

Joni was similarly motivated to keep learning and growing so we could run this race set before us. The Bible told us:

> Ask and it will be given to you; seek, and you will find; knock and the door will be opened to you. For everyone who asks receives; the one who seeks finds; and to the one who knocks, the door will be opened. (Matt. 7:7–8)

> If any of you lacks wisdom, you should ask God, who gives generously to all without finding fault, and it will be given to you. (James 1:5)

We lacked wisdom, therefore we asked, sought, and knocked.

I broke the binders of paperbacks, punched holes in their pages, and filled three-ringed notebooks that became a library of wisdom discovered by others who had run this race before us, seeking God, finding him, and becoming wiser.

"What should we read today, Jon?" I'd ask as we took our places at the dining room table paging through books—underlining, highlighting, discussing, devouring verses, and reading all the parallel passages.

Answers were hidden there, and we were determined to find them. We bought cassette tapes of emerging thinkers to learn from their insights on related topics. After listening intently to their inspirational stories, failures, and triumphs, we'd discuss the relevance of their conclusions to our struggles.

We sought out and attended seminars and workshops and listened to inspirational speakers, theologians, and trailblazers focused on knowing God and his purposes. We yearned to help and shepherd others through the trials and tribulations of life in a fallen world.

Joni and Jay attended a faith-healing extravaganza in Washington, DC, along with thousands of other hopeful souls. Why not?

"We want to check it out, Di."

"OK. But I'll stay here. I'm skeptical and suspect it's a money-making scam."

On another occasion, I drove to Philadelphia during a blinding blizzard with Joni and two friends to attend a three-day training event taught by Bill Bright, founder and director of Campus Crusade for Christ. His global vision to reach the world for Christ expanded our horizons beyond the farm and ourselves and would shape our individual ministry pursuits in years to come.

In the fall of 1969, Jay, Joni, and I drove to Philadelphia to attend The Institute in Basic Youth Conflicts,[1] written and presented by Bill Gothard. This week of teaching and training gave us the keys to unlock the Bible even further and glimpse the big picture God was painting of our lives.

During five full days of intensive instruction, several hundred people crowded into a small hotel conference room and soaked in powerful concepts and insights. He spoke while using a black marker to comment on multiple pages from our red binders projected onto a screen at the front of the room. He simplified core principles about success, self-image, commitment, family, rights, conscience, purpose, friends, freedom, and dating. I tried taking notes but couldn't keep up. He continued standing during breaks and meals, answering questions from long lines of attendees.

God's presence through his written word and his humble servant, Bill Gothard, permeated the room that week. Joni, Jay, and I returned to the farm with thick red binders packed with spiritual riches we still mine fifty years later. My original red notebook and handwritten notes reside on a shelf over my computer monitor for quick access. Joni's holds an identical place of honor in her office.

To this day, I divide my spiritual learning journey as pre- and post-Gothard. For twenty years leading up to his seminar, God had been tenderly fertilizing the soil of my spiritual life through family, friends, and church, but I still wasn't seeing and knowing myself as God did. Bill Gothard's insights and principles showed me it was time to plant new seeds and see what emerged. The sprouts began to reveal themselves in my prayers and self-talk:

God, thank you for how I look. The shape of my nose, my round face, and short neck. My big breasts. My large hands and long fingers. My thin ankles. My smile.

Thank you, God, for my parents. For their weaknesses. For their strengths. For the love they gave me.

Thank you for the brain you've given me. For its deficiencies and sufficiencies. Thank you for my voice and vocal cords that let me sing your praises. For eyes that see and ears that hear.

Thank you for providing everything I need—it is more than enough. Thank you, God, for the benefits of every irritation you allow in my life, great and small.

Forgive my whining and complaining, Lord.

Inject your strength into my frailties, Lord.

Mom, I forgive you for the lies. I forgive you for all the cakes and cookies you left that tempted me and for leaving me alone in front of the television and expecting me to take care of my sisters' needs. I forgive you for not being the mom I wanted and needed. I know you did the best you could. I'm sorry you ignored the love God wanted to pour out on you. I love you, Mom.

Dad, I forgive you for inappropriately touching me. I forgive you for withholding the affection and tenderness I needed as a child and teenager. I forgive you for not being the dad I wanted and needed. I know you did the best you could. I love you, Dad.

Lord, forgive me for measuring my success by what I am, compared to what I could be, or by what I do, compared to what I could be doing. Forgive me for ungratefulness, stubbornness, and bitterness.

Thanksgiving and forgiveness continued for months. I was learning about myself and my circumstances and, more importantly, about the sufficiency of God. Over the years I had repeatedly cried out, "Enough!" and now I was finding it was *God* who is enough.

PART 4

CHAPTER 16—READY, SET, GO

One day, a voice on the farm phone said, "We want to invite Joni to speak at our ladies' Bible study. Is she available?" This was Joni's first invitation to share her story! It was from a senior women's group that met in the basement of a Methodist church several miles away. When we arrived, I had to single-handedly lower Joni down a flight of marble stairs to the meeting room and pull her back up when we left.

Note to self: First, check out all the logistics of any invitation before saying yes! Second, insist on a fully accessible room if this ever happens again.

I had jotted Joni's notes on a crumpled piece of paper and placed it on her knee. As I listened from the back of the room, my heart soared, not because of the content or the emotions her presence evoked, but because I could foresee that the message God spoke through her that day about faith and suffering would deepen and grow over time to enrich and bless all who would hear or read it.

Joni's ministry was also expanding through another of her gifts. At Rancho Los Amigos Rehab in California, Joni had learned to draw, paint, and write with a pen or brush in her mouth. At home, she spent time at an easel with a pencil or black felt-tip pen clenched between her teeth. She drew familiar themes like horses, skiers, rustic cabins, and mountain ranges.

"Hey, let's print copies of your drawings and try to sell them," someone suggested.

"We'll need a catalog," I added.

"Who can we find to do this?" said another.

"We can do it," I answered. "Why not?"

We designed a tri-fold catalog with an order form and printed a small quantity of prints and catalogs. Later, we took these when Joni spoke and offered them for sale. As the original drawings accumulated, Mr. Eareckson matted them and made rustic frames. Three years later, another friend arranged an art exhibit of these originals at a local coffee shop. A companion article appeared in the Baltimore *News American*,[1] and Mayor William Donald Schaefer proclaimed February 4–10, 1973, as "Joni Eareckson Week."

My days were filled with studying, caring for Joni, enjoying our rich friendship and fellowship, interacting with an assortment of friends and visitors throughout the evenings at the farm, and imagining what the future might hold for each of us. Joni's days were filled with reading, studying, drawing, and flexing her spiritual muscles through prayer and discussion, and developing lifelong friendships with a growing group of faithful friends.

Throughout the week, Jay did the cooking, cleaning, entertaining, and caring for Joni. Her evenings and weekends were usually free as I and other friends filled in any gaps in Joni's twenty-four/seven care.

Apparently, we didn't have enough on our plates because Allen, an ambitious high school friend, approached Joni and me to help form a band. He was a songwriter and remembered us from choir. Joni sang soprano, and I sang alto. Allen also approached two other mutual friends—Chuck, a guitarist/ bass singer, and his brother Craig, a bass player/tenor. "Great idea. Sounds like fun. Let's do it!" we all said.

We performed at private church parties, coffee houses, assemblies, and impromptu concerts, and even went to a recording studio to make a few demos. Who knew at the time that even this larky adventure was preparation for Joni's own musical cassettes, records, and other assorted recordings?

Remarkably, she received an Academy Award nomination, albeit brief, for best song, "Alone, Yet Not Alone," which she recorded for a full-length movie of the same name in 2013.

As 1970 ended, things were looking up. Joni was regaining her resilience. Depression was slowly becoming a thing of the past. She was gaining local attention, and promising possibilities appeared on the horizon. For me, an intensive mini-mester of four credits and my final spring semester packed with twenty credits, including student teaching at Woodlawn High School, took me across the academic finish line to win the coveted bachelor's degree at last.

Leaving my parents' home had been a necessary transition when I turned eighteen. Emancipation from the constant emotional oppression freed my mind, heart, and spirit to nurture new life and possibilities. But I did regret not spending more quality time with Jessie and Cassie, who were still trapped in the chaos.

I began to take incremental steps, in manageable chunks, to reconnect with Mom. During summer break, I would occasionally take Joni over to our pool to float on an inflatable raft, enjoy Heidi our dog, sip sodas through a long straw, and work on her tan. Jessie and Cassie were a great help tending to Joni's needs, and they had fun becoming friends with her.

As soon as Jessie was old enough to attend a Gothard Seminar, I took her. Cassie attended one the following year. I attended their important events: singing, acting, dance recitals, sports games, etc. I overlapped at church when possible. Heidi stood guard day and night. Dad kept working and paid my college tuition. Mom? Well, Mom continued her clandestine affair with Hank, effectively abandoning Jessie and Cassie in their most formative years. This would create incalculable havoc for decades.

CHAPTER 17—THE YEAR OF YOUNG LOVE

On an ordinary day in January 1971, I was visiting my mom when the phone rang. "It's for you," Mom said as she handed the receiver to me.

The caller was Tom. I had briefly met him in 1967 when we both had summer jobs at the Christian Admiral Hotel in Cape May. He worked the bakery night shift and slept most of the day, so our paths rarely crossed. In 1970, his family had moved from Delaware to Baltimore where his father became pastor of what was left of the original South Baltimore Bible Presbyterian Church. Having recently graduated with a bachelor of arts in aeronautical engineering, Tom had joined the rest of the family in their modest home while he looked for employment.

"Hi," Tom said over the phone. "I graduated from college last month and am currently living with my parents in Baltimore. I'd like to start dating. Do you know anyone I could call? Let me know if you do. Thanks."

I was civil on the phone, but after Tom hung up, I vented to Mom, "What a jerk! This guy is clueless. Remind me to forget about him!"

Mom made the fateful suggestion: "You don't have anything better to do, right? Call him back and see if he'd like to take you out."

Why did I listen to her? Boredom? Hormones? Loneliness? I've had fifty years to ruminate on it and have no solid explanation.

I called Tom back.

"Hey, I know a girl you could take out on a date. Me."

Immediately embarrassed, he apologized profusely and asked me out. We went to the circus and had a nice time. During January, we saw each other daily in between my caring for Joni, student teaching, and taking classes, and Tom's job searching. One of Dad's friends recommended Tom for an engineering job with Baltimore City. By the end of the month, he was employed.

On February 1, he proposed. I impetuously accepted.

Neither of us was prepared for this commitment. He was on an emotional rebound from being rejected by his college sweetheart. He wanted to be married and get on with life. I had never dated and was an inexperienced, needy young woman. I was committed to following all the principles I had learned from Scripture, Bill Gothard, and years of living with a mother who modeled what not to do.

We talked a lot in the beginning. I shared the essence of my childhood struggles, how God had loved me through them, and what I had learned because of them. Tom shared a few of his childhood struggles too. Sadly, as he began to talk about his childhood, I discovered that being a preacher's kid had had a negative impact on him.

"Go up front, Tommy, go up front," his mother whispered insistently during the church service as she jabbed her index finger into his back. "It's time you went forward to make a decision for Christ." Tom silently and secretly fumed. *I will not go up. I will decide if and when I make that decision.*

A handful of old folks gathered for years in the family's living room for Wednesday night prayer meetings. "Sit down and be quiet, kids. It's time for prayer meeting to begin," said Thomas Sr., directing his five children. Tom learned well how to feign outward compliance while storing up inward rebellion. Earnest prayerful petitions droned on endlessly as Tom unwillingly endured the boredom of his father's forced expectations.

How could I have fully understood that the inevitable consequences of Tom's stubborn attitude toward his parents' requests, his prideful resistance to God, and his repudiation of prayer would become lifelong deadweights on his heart and mind? They became baked-in habits of passive-aggressive resistance that inhibited him from learning from the past, adapting to change, persevering, or flourishing over time.

We hardly knew each other but thought we knew it all. Whatever might need fixing, I was sure I could do it. I was good at that. I'm the one who runs into burning buildings!

$$\mathcal{D}$$

We picked June 26 for the big day and planned a Bermuda honeymoon. Wedding planning added to my already ambitious schedule, but my adrenaline was sky high, and sleep became unimportant. I was swept away by the fantasy of living happily ever after. My prince had come to rescue me from loneliness, poverty, insecurity, and uncertainty.

More than two hundred family and friends rejoiced with us on our wedding day, hopeful that the next chapter in our lives would be happy and blessed. Finger food, punch, and a four-tier cake worked for Dad's tight budget, and a good time was had by all. Thankfully, Mom behaved herself.

Thomas Sr. officiated the ceremony. He hadn't offered us any premarital counseling or words of wisdom. I learned years later that in the vestry, waiting for me to come down the aisle, Senior told Junior it wasn't too late to call off the wedding if he wanted to change his mind. Recently, I asked Tom why his father made those comments. Apparently, he and Martha didn't believe I was Bible Presbyterian enough.

It came as no surprise when I recalled how Thomas Sr. and my soon-to-be mother-in-law, Martha, responded to our engagement announcement. They were seated in easy chairs in their living room reading the evening newspaper when we shared our happy news and waited for hugs and well wishes all around. Instead, they remained motionless, eyes glued to their newspapers for what seemed like fifteen minutes of silence. Feeling very awkward, we looked at each other, shrugged our shoulders, and walked out. Nothing was said then or later. At the time, I told myself I wasn't marrying them, I was marrying Thomas Jr., right?

Many family and friends did more than we could have imagined to help us begin our marriage on a solid foundation, literally. Prior to the wedding, Mr. Eareckson offered Tom and me a generous gift of one acre across from the farm on River Road and included a personal loan for us to build our home there. Short-term, he invited us to live in another house on the property until we finished building ours. He foresaw the mutual benefit for both families with such an arrangement, particularly for Joni. Flabbergasted, Tom and I talked it over and accepted Mr. Eareckson's plan.

Tom went back to work after the honeymoon. In the evenings, we began to design and then build our home on River Road.

CHAPTER 18—A TIME TO LAUGH

Our married life found its rhythm. After sending my hubby off early in the morning and preplanning dinner, I packed a small lunch, gathered what was needed for the day, and walked across the footpath between our temporary home and Jay's house.

"Morning, Jay. Hi, Joni. Coffee ready?"

"Hi, Di!" they both yelled. "Come on in!"

We'd talk and sing and chat through Joni's hour-long morning routine until she was upright in the chair, all beautified, ready to eat breakfast, and greet the day full speed ahead.

"Where did we stop in this book yesterday, Di? Let's start there," she gestured with her braced arm.

Positioning the book on the table, I replied, "OK! Let's do it."

Joni and I continued to examine Bible commentaries and other works of contemporary theologians and authors to enhance our understanding of life—particularly focusing on the apparent paradoxes of pain and suffering juxtaposed with God's love and his will for our lives. We painstakingly put the pieces of the puzzle together. Occasionally Steve Estes would join us.

I had met Steve in high school through his sister. I had grown to know and love the entire Estes family, attending their church and joining its young adult group. Steve was passionate about his faith walk. He was a sponge soaking in spiritual insights and a serious truth seeker. I knew he and Joni would enjoy getting to know each other and benefit from unpacking her penetrating questions together. He began to stop by the farm several times a week to dig deeply into God's Word with Joni.

I walked home around 5:00 p.m. each weekday afternoon, prepared dinner, and looked forward to evenings with Tom. I usually assisted Jay with Joni's morning and bedtime routines on weekends. Other friends occasionally came to give us a break.

During this time, several unanticipated things were also happening in Joni's life and mine. At the prompting of one of Mr. Eareckson's business friends, the *Baltimore News American* sent a reporter to interview Joni. The article, "Paralyzed Girl Goes to College," appeared on September 1, 1969. It was followed by a short TV interview on WBAL local news.

Local media interviews and speaking invitations increased after that bit of publicity. I was the designated chauffer, photographer, historian, and appointment secretary. I began to organize the calendar, arrange travel logistics, and manage the secretarial and correspondence needs. Sensing even more growth to come, I started a scrapbook and photo collection to archive the milestones on this marathon as they whizzed by.

Tom and I began the construction of our spacious new house in the fall of 1972. We built the house to cut construction costs. We hired sub-contractors for the big things and did most of the smaller jobs ourselves. I helped smooth out the poured concrete for the basement floor, set the long steel beam on a cinderblock wall and a steel pole, and hammered asphalt tiles onto the tarpapered plywood roof while tethered to the apex. (I am afraid of heights!) I installed all the insulation in the attic and exterior walls and drilled peg holes in the random-width oak flooring in the living room, dining room, and hallway. Tom and I were a good team.

When it was time to move into our new home, all our belongings were transported from the temporary house to the new one on a rickety old hay wagon pulled by Mr. Eareckson's ancient International tractor. Mom was precariously perched in a chair on top of our meager earthly possessions. It was quite a day!

I found marriage very pleasurable and satisfying, including the physical part. I purposely wanted a full-sized bed. Anything bigger placed us further apart. Closeness was soothing and reassuring to me. I enjoyed Tom's companionship. We took weekend sightseeing trips, joined a church, and enjoyed making our house a home even though our financial resources were thin. He designed and built bookshelves and TV centers, finished off the basement, and added rustic timbers and moldings where needed. We were at our best when working together to maintain and enhance our home.

Dad won $5,000 at a local raffle. Mom convinced him to take the family, including Tom and me, for an all-expenses-paid week in Bermuda, his father's birthplace. We had many relatives on the island and enjoyed meeting them. But the highlight of the week was deciding it was time for us to start a family. A month later, my pregnancy was confirmed. We were elated and began to design the nursery.

Could a heart ever be so full of joy as mine? I was twenty-five, happily married, expecting my first child, and the owner of a new home surrounded by tall locust trees on the crest of a hill overlooking the meandering Patapsco River. Although sparsely decorated with used furniture rescued from the landfill, our home was bursting with new love, new life, big dreams, and high expectations.

At sunrise and sunset, I often recited Psalm 23 as I sat at the graying picnic table at the crest of the hill behind our home. "He guides me along the right paths for his name's sake" (v. 3) especially stood out as I ruminated on what God was fashioning from the ashes of Joni's life and mine. Together, we had become dreamers of big dreams, believing that he would bring beauty out of our brokenness. Could it be that the long season of mourning and despair had passed, and the splendor of the Lord was going to be displayed in two broken reeds of flesh named Di and Joni?

I could barely breathe it all in.

CHAPTER 19—FULL HOUSE

Pregnancy was uneventful except for the nausea and vomiting. I especially hated the dry heaving. My tummy got big and round. I gained forty pounds in nine months. I sensed disapproval in Tom's facial expressions and correctly perceived they were focused on my weight gain. But pregnant women gain weight. What's the big deal? The extra pounds can come off after delivery.

Delivery day arrived on June 15, 1974, after twenty-four hours of extended, painful labor. A C-section was considered, but after a few aggressive pushes on my belly to reposition the baby, Andrew was born with a temporary, red-tipped conehead from all the pushing. He weighed seven pounds, eight ounces and was twenty-one inches long. Fathers and other family weren't allowed into the labor and delivery rooms back then, but I knew one of the attending nurses from the South Baltimore church. *Thank you, Jesus, for that kind, familiar face in the delivery room!*

This new joy was like no other. The miracle of life, the exquisite handiwork of God knowing Andrew and knitting him together in my womb (Ps. 139:13) changed our lives forever.

𝒟

In between feeding and cuddling Andy, changing diapers, making dinner, and doing laundry, I quickly learned how to improve my multi-tasking work habits. During the day, I set up a playpen/play area to care for and enjoy Andy in Jay's dining room while also assisting Joni.

My responsibilities as a new mom had to be integrated around the ever-expanding demands of Joni's growing reputation. It quickly became obvious we needed a business to handle all the logistics of producing, marketing, advertising, and shipping Joni's artwork. Mr. Merriman, father of a high school friend, became our trusted lawyer and made us legal. We became official as Joni Unlimited, Inc., a Maryland corporation with fifty-fifty ownership between Joni and me. He recommended an accountant who taught me how to do basic bookkeeping with paper and pencil on ledger sheets. We didn't have computers or cell phones then.

The first order of prints and catalogs arrived at my backdoor. *Shazam!* Our third bedroom became a warehouse and shipping room. The overhead was low. Free.

The farm phone and my phone began to ring more often. Requests for Joni to speak came from local Christian groups, women's clubs, Young Life clubs, local churches, and more. Several women from our close circle of friends joined the support team with Jay and me to supplement home-care hours and be companions at speaking engagements.

Joni began to spend most weekends at our house, so I wouldn't need to run up and down the driveway to assist with her care. Her father set up a manually operated hospital bed in our third bedroom. She came to church with us. Many friends picked her up to do fun things that engaged her in life away from the farm.

Our house was filling up.

One night in 1974, Dad finally got in touch with reality and discovered Mom's sordid decade-long affair. Unexpectedly alone together at Chisholm Drive on that horrible evening, he looked me in the eyes and asked, "Have you known about your mother's affair with Hank the whole time?"

I was silent.

"Now I understand how one man can kill another," Dad said.

With that, he calmly left. He disappeared for a few days, eventually returning for his things while Mom was at work. He filed for divorce. Then he called me.

"Diana, it would help if I could live at your house for a while, until I pay off my debts."

"Sure, Dad," I responded. "We'll fix up a spare bedroom for you downstairs. Come." He stayed for four years, working day and night to pay off all the debts Mom had accumulated over the years.

Our house became even fuller, but there was still room for more.

$\mathcal{D}$

On September 11, 1974, Barbara Walters interviewed Joni between 7:15 a.m. and 7:30 a.m. in NBC's New York studio. Joni had become a national celebrity. What next?

The managing editor of the book division at Zondervan, a Christian publishing house, called.

"We saw your *Today* interview yesterday and want to publish your story."

A Gillette Company/Paper Mate Division public relations representative called. "The president of the company admired your story and noticed you were drawing with Paper Mate's felt-tip pen in your mouth. Gillette wants to sponsor three major art exhibits of your mouth-drawings in New York, Chicago, and Los Angeles. Our public relations firm will do all the setup including travel, lodging, multimedia interviews, and publicity."

Pastors from Kansas, Phoenix, and Toronto called. "Please come and share your testimony with our congregations."

Bill Gothard wrote a warm letter to Joni, glorifying God with her.

An executive from Hershey Chocolate World called. "Please come speak to our boys at the Hershey School and also the Evangelical Free Church in town."

It was time to expand the kitchen table operation to manage new opportunities emerging daily. Our large basement became Joni Unlimited headquarters. Tom constructed shelving units and shipping benches. We ordered a bigger supply of matted art prints and purchased used office furniture, telephones, desks, chairs, lamps, and office supplies. We hired Carol and two other Woodlawn Young Life friends to fill orders. The new home team went into action.

A small area was set up for those of us with children. Playpens, doorway jump-ups, and Big Wheels kept them busy. Sippy cups, coffee pots, and bag lunches kept the troops fed and watered. Oh, we were a merry band of workers on a mighty mission in a basement at the top of a hill on River Road. A full house and full hearts!

CHAPTER 20—HOME TEAMS

I learned to be a more effective general manager for Joni Unlimited having observed a professional public relations firm in action. I became proficient at responding to incoming requests, tracking inventories and finances, supervising employees, and coordinating objectives and goals to maximize Joni's time and stamina and multiple peoples' schedules, including my family's. It was like producing and directing a Broadway blockbuster.

My UMBC theater courses in acting and directing, producing, and promoting would finally be good for something!

From December 1974 through December 1975, I traveled, when available, with Joni and our other trained caregiving friends, as her manager and traveling companion. Together, we embarked on a multi-media blitz, traveling to fourteen states for forty-two speaking engagements and seven art exhibits.

The first show was at a prestigious art gallery in Chicago where nineteen of Joni's originals were on exhibit. The public relations agent escorted us through a whirlwind media blitz of the Windy City including TV, radio, newspaper, and magazine interviews.

Jay, Joni, and I also traveled to California to exhibit her artwork in central Los Angeles. More TV, radio, and newspaper interviews. Then, almost a month later, Joni,

Bonnie, and I flew to New York City for another art exhibit and media interviews at Lincoln Center.

At each location, we sold artwork and had a jolly old time doing it. We took lots of photographs, and I later archived each trip and event with photos and media articles.

As art sales grew, our need for space grew. Joni and I decided to rent three floors of warehouse space in Sykesville. They became home to inventory storage, shipping and receiving, and office/nursery/lunchroom/communication operations. We built more shelving and bought a computer for the bulging mailing list and a shrink-wrap machine to package Joni's matted prints.

We were now shipping artwork all over the country to Christian bookstores and thousands of individuals. Suddenly, we had nine employees at the warehouse and other volunteers traveling with Joni.

Joni couldn't keep up with the need for new artwork. Plus, we needed to add colorful items to enhance our market presence beyond the demand for black-and-white. We searched for new artists, preferably disabled, but didn't find anyone whose work matched the quality needed. Bonnie, my childhood friend, was a gifted watercolor artist. We asked her to submit greeting card designs with Bible verses and Christian messages. We loved them. We decided to repackage Joni's black-and-white designs into greeting cards also. In a few months, we had a color catalogue of Joni's and Bonnie's greeting cards, framed and matted prints, tote bags, wooden plaques, and more. I designed a new four-color catalog with Joni, pencil in mouth at her easel, on the cover. Sales boomed with Bonnie's cards eventually outselling Joni's.

We asked Julie, another Young Life friend, to join the home team as Joni's administrative assistant and traveling companion. I couldn't sustain Joni's daily caregiving and appointment calendar and effectively manage the ever-expanding Joni Unlimited while simultaneously loving my husband, parenting Andy, and caring for our home. In addition, I was still experiencing collateral damage from my parents' dramas.

☎

While the Joni Unlimited home team was functioning beautifully, my personal home team was in trouble.

After Andy's birth, Tom's dysfunctional habits increasingly intruded into our lives.

Work bored him. Occasionally he took naps at the office. I became alarmed. He didn't like traffic design engineering and didn't want to move up the ladder at the office. His income stagnated, and our financial struggle worsened. I suggested my father's profession, piano tuning, but Tom said, "I wouldn't enjoy that."

He eventually left the traffic design engineering job and opened the Village Gallery when a prominent property owner offered him one year, rent free, in a quaint storefront on Main Street, Sykesville. He matted and framed Joni's prints, sold original artwork and limited-edition prints from local and other well-known artists, and did typical picture framing with a flair for decorative matting. He found a new sense of purpose in doing his part to expand and support Joni's ministry to people with disabilities.

Tom had always struggled to make friends. As that continued, he became more isolated. A story he had told me when we were dating often came to my mind:

"Tommy, you can't go outside until you make your bed and clean your room," may seem like a reasonable request from a mother to a son, but to Tom it was an onerous command under any circumstance. He didn't like to make his bed or clean up his room and wouldn't obey even if it meant he never went outside on the weekends. Well, that's what happened. He spent his childhood in his room on the weekends, doing what he chose to do.

The self-imposed isolation of Tom's defiant decisions hindered him from learning healthy interpersonal skills. As a married adult, he avoided social gatherings, small-group activities, and Bible studies. I went to most social occasions alone.

He could stay in his room, but I was going to grow and live and flourish.

He was also a slob, firmly entrenched in his childhood rebellion, and refused to pick up or clean up any mess he made. It became a constant point of contention between us in every room in the house.

When Tom first began to withdraw from the marriage and from me during my pregnancy, I guessed it was because of my weight. I was painfully aware of his gradual withdrawal and fixed what was causing it by losing the pounds I'd gained during pregnancy. Yet his nonverbal messages were making it unmistakably clear that I was the problem. If I would "blank," our relationship would improve. I didn't know how to fill in the blank, and over time, my self-esteem hit bottom under his constant criticism and shaming.

I was getting older and still wanted to have another child. Purposing to lose weight before trying to become pregnant again, I unexpectedly discovered I was pregnant. I was elated.

Michael, a ten-pound bundle of joy, was born August 10, 1978, after another lengthy labor and delivery. We moved Andy into the larger bedroom, which he shared with Joni on the weekends, and Mike got the nursery. Soon after his second grandson's birth, Dad moved out of the basement and in with his new wife, Lizzy. More about that later.

Michael's arrival did nothing to improve the relationship between Tom and me. I longed for our boys to have healthy role models. I dreaded the horror of reliving my parents' nightmare marriage.

How could this be happening to me? God, where are you? Why don't you answer my prayers? Rescue me! Help me! Please!

My life with Tom began to feel like an invisible detention center where I waited for the daily verdict: guilty or innocent, sentenced or released.

CHAPTER 21—NATIONAL BESTSELLER

Our youthful can-do attitude compelled us to try writing Joni's story ourselves after Zondervan expressed interest in publishing Joni's story. By phone and in person, I started to interview friends and acquaintances involved in Joni's life since the diving accident to establish an accurate timeline of events and identify foundational themes of the post-accident story. Once finished, Joni and I began to write. Zondervan asked for samples of our efforts, which were periodically mailed for their review. To broaden our perspective they sent us popular autobiographies.

Two months of effort were revealing. The task was too big for us, it would take too long, and we lacked the skills and experience to produce the best outcome.

Joni, Jay, and I flew to Zondervan's headquarters in Grand Rapids, Michigan, to meet the managing editor and the executive vice president of the book division. An agreement to publish Joni's story was reached. We got a tour of the new computerized warehouse and met several ghostwriter possibilities. Joe Musser was ultimately selected to write the book.

Joni and I sat with Joe Musser at Jay's dining room table with my timelines and copious notes. Joe pushed the record button, and we spoke into the microphone. Several days later, after hours of animated, emotional conversation from

Joni, me, Jay, Mr. Eareckson, and Steve Estes, the storytelling came to a close. Joe returned to Illinois to memorialize it on paper.

Busy schedules continued until the manuscript arrived. Gathering at the table, we eagerly devoured the pages.

"Jon, this is good, really good."

"This can't be printed, Di. It needs to go back."

"Why?"

"Not enough said about my family's involvement."

"OK. Back it goes. Call him and share your suggestions."

Several weeks later the second manuscript arrived. Again, we excitedly read each page. Approved.

In July 1976, Zondervan launched a *Joni* multi-media campaign. The book became an immediate bestseller. By December, 1.7 million people had viewed or received Zondervan's ads, and many others met Joni at twenty-two book-signing parties across the country.

Early in the process, I had asked Zondervan to put Joni Unlimited's Sykesville address on the book jacket. Now, the local post office was inundated with large canvas bags stuffed with hundreds of letters addressed to Joni. People wanted to buy her book and purchase her artwork. Many others poured out their hearts with their own stories seeking answers to their questions and requesting prayer. Obviously, Joni could not respond to this volume of personal mail.

What to do?

After focused prayer and discussion, we approached Aunt Blanche. She had been retired for a few years but was still a wellspring of wisdom, knowledge, and experience.

Would she personally answer these letters for Joni?

She came to the farm. We chatted, laughed, and prayed, and she happily and gratefully agreed. This was an answer to our prayers and hers. She had been searching for meaningful ways to continue loving and helping needy people in her remaining years. She had found what she was seeking.

We developed a few standard replies to Joni's correspondence, but Aunt Blanche personally answered thousands of letters by hand on lovely stationery. This worked well until Blanche's death in 1978. Another wise senior saint from our church continued responding to these letters until her own passing.

In the fall of 1977, Zondervan showcased *Joni* at the annual Christian Booksellers Convention in Kansas City where thousands of Christian bookstore owners, salespeople, and publishers gathered. Joni Unlimited had its own booth to promote and sell Joni and Bonnie prints and greeting cards. For the next two years, one third of our annual orders and sales were generated from this event.

The recent publication of the twenty-fifth edition of *Joni* marks sales of more than three million books in forty languages.

Gillette's public relations firm had lots of clients. Greyhound was one of them. They were rolling out a new program in the public transportation/coach industry called Helping Hand. Would Joni be interested in becoming a travel consultant for this program by going on bus tours around the country? A robust companion media campaign would highlight the Helping Hand program and Joni's book and artwork.

Yes.

Joni and her traveling companions began touring designated bus routes between June and Labor Day, 1976. The tour coincided with Zondervan's July kickoff of her book and maximized her media exposure. I worked with all parties to integrate bus tour dates and multi-city/state locations with overlapping, prearranged engagements on Joni's calendar. Joni thrived on the tour.

Another employee/friend and I joined Joni on the Seattle, San Francisco, and Phoenix trips. We rolled in and out of TV and radio studios, met newspaper reporters and photographers, and squeezed in personal sightseeing and photo shoots. Sadly, while we were in Tacoma, Washington, Aunt Blanche passed away, and we couldn't attend her memorial service.

That year our rotating teams wheeled Joni through twenty-three newspaper, nine magazine, and thirty-five live radio interviews; thirty-four TV appearances, eighty-six speaking engagements, two art exhibits, and twenty-two book parties.

If we expected a less hectic 1977, we were wrong. That year included four newspaper articles, three magazine features, five TV appearances, three radio interviews, sixty-five speaking engagements, an art exhibit, and fourteen book-signing parties. Perhaps my favorite moment was March 2, 1977. I was present during Joni's live *Good Morning America* interview with David Hartman.

I loved that show.

Another favorite was meeting two of my childhood heroes, Roy Rogers and Dale Evans, in Los Angeles at a muscular dystrophy telethon. I could hardly believe it. Roy and Dale! They were gracious and spent a few precious moments chatting with me off stage.

I sang "Happy Trails to You, Until We Meet Again" for days until my companions had had enough.

Another milestone. On June 4, 1978, Joni began her first international book and artwork promotion and speaking tour in Europe. She traveled to Switzerland, Germany, Sweden, Scotland, England, and Norway accompanied by her sisters Jay and Kathy and another administrative assistant. She returned to Baltimore on July 9.

CHAPTER 22—JONI PTL IS BORN

Our next adventure began with Joni's first appearance on Youth Night, August 21, 1976, at a Billy Graham Crusade televised on WEAU-TV from Pontiac Metropolitan Stadium in southeast Michigan.

Afterward, the Graham organization approached Joni to consider letting them make a feature film of her story. Would she fly with Jay and Jessie to the World Wide Pictures studio in Burbank, California, to film a screen test? She did. She was perfect for the part.

Production and filming of the movie *Joni* would begin in August 1978, and we had a lot of decisions to make and planning to work through before then.

"Joni, I have lots of ideas scribbled down on paper that I would like to discuss with you."

My creative developer mind was racing ahead, as usual, identifying different scenarios for each new challenge that would accompany the ministry expansion that was sure to follow the movie's planned release a year later in 1979.

As executive director of Joni Unlimited, Inc., I had reached out to Bill Gothard, Joe Musser, several other mentors, and our existing Joni Unlimited team to discuss a multitude of possibilities. The consensus was that we should form a nonprofit organization.

Joni and I discussed many exciting possibilities: counseling services and referrals; the production of tapes, films, radio, and TV programs; training seminars; periodical publications; education modules and literature of all types; forming evangelistic teams to multiply the message and impact; and on and on. We also discussed broad goals and objectives, a charter, and a possible board of directors, and chose a name, The Joni PTL Ministry, Inc. We discussed sources of future income to support such a national and international outreach. With more details on paper, legal and practical logistics could proceed without delay, sandwiched between all her comings and goings.

Other practical considerations involved how to responsibly hire, acquire, and manage all the additional skills, resources, personnel, and equipment it would take to successfully launch a nonprofit organization functioning alongside Joni Unlimited. I began planning how to meet the most pressing and obvious needs of the print and stationery company.

I had asked Tom to join me at the warehouse to cover areas in which he excelled, and I was weak when he left his city job and opened the Village Gallery. I had worn too many hats for too many years and couldn't do it all anymore. He subbed for me caring for Michael and provided practical support for our daily operations. But there was more he could do for the art company.

When I discussed this with Joni, she wasn't sure it was a good idea. She assumed we didn't have the money. I reminded her that Tom had already prepared forms, created fliers, constructed an exhibit booth from weathered barn siding, picked up and unloaded hundreds of boxes of inventory into the warehouse and more. He did all this without pay while running his art gallery and picture-framing shop. I hoped to make his part-time role official by paying him a minimal wage for his efforts.

Joni and I agreed to disagree. Tom's responsibilities grew with Joni's reservations noted. We would monitor the situation and review it in six months.

In July 1978, Tom and I loaded up the Joni Unlimited van with our convention exhibit, art inventory, order forms, promotional material, etc. and drove to Denver. The rest of the home team flew in with Joni and helped set up and handle sales at our exhibit at the Christian Booksellers Convention. Her second book, *A Step Further*, co-written with Steve Estes, was to be launched. It was an electrifying four days on the convention floor. After packing up the exhibit booth, the team flew home. Tom, my sister Jessie, and I remained with Joni.

On July 12, Joni wheeled onto the Red Rocks Amphitheater stage to speak to a sold-out crowd. It had been raining, but now the rumbling black clouds were moving on. A gentle breeze greeted her as dusk descended, and the spotlights came on among the impressive red cliffs. It was awesome.

The next day, Joni, Tom, Jessie, and I drove to Denver International Airport where Joni boarded a plane headed to Burbank and the World Wide Pictures movie studio. We met Judy, an employee of the Billy Graham Evangelistic Association, at the boarding gate. She would accompany Joni to Los Angeles for the filming of the movie on August 14 and continue on as her new caregiver/companion during the production phase of the film. In addition to loaning Judy to Joni, the Graham organization had rented a house, an electric wheelchair, and an accessible van.

A quiet round of hushed prayers consecrated this extraordinary moment. Hugs were given and received. Joni and I lingered in our embrace, neither wanting to let go of the other. Tears of sadness and joy flowed. Joy, because we were confident God was doing great things beyond our mortal comprehension. That our broken vessels had been chosen to be part of his cosmic plan. We were humbled and awed by his great love and grace.

"I love you, Jon."

"I love you too, Di."

I watched Judy push Joni down the gateway until they disappeared into the plane. I had a haunting premonition that unanticipated changes would propel all of us in unknown directions. A memory came to mind of the note Joni had written in my personal copy of the first edition of *Joni* in July 1976:

"Di, Our dearest friendship, partnership in providence for the advancement of Christ's gospel, and companionship in the most glorious ministry! Love, Joni."

Having experienced all God had done in our lives so far, I chose to believe all would continue uninterrupted.

While Joni was in Burbank, I was actively preparing for a surge of demand for her prints, greeting cards, and other items when the movie was released I spent many hours with our wonderful printer in Baltimore, finalizing all the details of what to print, quantities, packaging, catalog design, and promotional photos. At the same time, Joni, Bonnie, and I were finalizing new designs, internal greetings, and the accompanying verses for their artwork.

Tom was ordering matting and framing supplies for filling orders for Joni's prints. He built more shelving for the inventory on the lower floor of the warehouse. Carol was ordering all other supplies we needed in the fulfillment center. Our technical guy was maintaining the ever-expanding mailing list, payroll calculations, and keeping the computer in good working order. I was also working on accounts receivable and payable, and consulting with our accountant about IRS reports, budgeting, and financial projections for the next three to five years for Joni Unlimited, Inc. and Joni PTL Ministries, Inc.

Tom also initiated a midyear bulk sales promotion with special pricing for all our wholesale buyers across the country. The fulfillment center employees were working at full capacity, and I was considering extra help for the upcoming holiday season.

We never incurred any debt but plowed the profits into year-end employee bonuses and back into the business for the eagerly awaited expansion. We did, however, have accounts payable with the printer and other suppliers that we were confident we could pay off as usual.

Altogether, ten members of the home team remained in Sykesville during this time. We were buzzing with excitement, anticipating the release of the movie and what that would surely mean for all of us. Several gals on the home team rotated in and out of Los Angeles as volunteer caregivers to assist Judy. I spent two weeks with them during which I met Billy Graham as he watched from behind the camera one afternoon.

By November 20, 1978, our lawyer had submitted all the necessary paperwork to the State of Maryland, and we became an official non-profit corporation under Maryland law. He continued to write the bylaws and filed for tax exemption for Joni PTL Ministry, Inc. On April 26, 1979, he sent another letter clarifying changes we suggested for the Article III—Board of Directors Bylaws. He was awaiting our final review and approval.

CHAPTER 23 — THAT'S A WRAP

Joni, accompanied by Jay, returned to the farm in the fall of 1978 to film the last scenes of the movie in Baltimore and its suburbs, including Sykesville where colorful leaves blanketed the gravel paths and hillsides. The final scene was filmed at the crest of the Eareckson's gently rolling horse pasture adjacent to our home. Joni's East and West Coast friends and support teams gathered on the hill that beautiful day sipping coffee, eating donuts, and clicking cameras. We surrounded a huge camera platform hoisted high in the air and mounted on a flatbed truck anchored to the ground.

"Take One. Camera rolling."

Joni appears out of the tree line in the distance in her electric wheelchair slowly rolling through the hay field to the top of the hill. Music plays as she sings the movie theme song, "Journey's End."

"That's a wrap!"

Cheering and applause erupted. Hugs and tears filled the moment. It was finished. We witnessed a special moment in time that continues to be replayed all over the world forty years later. We were inspired, awed, grateful, and full of praise to God for his goodness and love. Unforgettable!

Jay, Joni's sister, and Ben, the assistant director of the movie, surprised us all by announcing their engagement. The wedding ceremony took place in Jay's living room immediately after the last scene was in the can. It was October 27, 1978.

The small group of friends, family, and crew gathered around the couple. They spoke their vows. Ben kissed his new bride. The crew disbanded, packed up their equipment, and drove off waving best wishes out van windows. We watched as they disappeared around the sharp curve winding up River Road.

Joni's home team personal assistant resumed her role, and I continued as executive director of Joni Unlimited and interim director of Joni PTL Ministries.

On the surface, it seemed like business as usual, but significant changes had occurred. Joni had lived in Los Angeles long enough to experience new feelings of freedom and independence. She had been given an electric wheelchair, Judy's watchful caregiving, and an apartment of her own where she discovered the joy of being her thirty-year-old self. Joni had become a mature, talented woman contemplating a promising future with new optimism and aspirations.

Now, Joni's electric wheelchair was parked in the shed. Jay's home was multilevel with two, three, and four steps between each interior room and the exterior doors and driveway. Consequently, Joni was stationary in her manual wheelchair once again. Such restricted mobility was a sharp contrast to the mobility she had enjoyed in Los Angeles.

Tom and I were located opposite their horse barn on River Road and up a steep driveway through the trees at the top of the hill. The Joni Unlimited warehouse was two miles down River Road, across the Patapsco River Bridge and next to the railroad depot in Sykesville.

Joni and I began to establish a new functional equilibrium and carry on with the urgent business of two enterprises, Joni

Unlimited, Inc. and Joni PTL Ministries. We adapted as best we could as circumstances changed. We moved our planning and work time to phone conferences, the warehouse, or my house. I encouraged her to consider building her own home in the Eareckson's hay field adjacent to our home. Or to buy or build a new home for herself in Sykesville. It became increasingly difficult to manage the number of rapidly changing circumstances. I could sense Joni's physical and emotional struggle without the electric wheelchair, but problem-solver that I was, I didn't know how to solve this one.

$\mathcal{D}$

One fateful day, I got a phone call from Julie, one of Joni's frequent caregiver/traveling companions. "Hi, Di. Joni will be in Hershey tomorrow evening speaking to the student body and faculty at the Hershey School for Boys. Could you and Tom come early and meet over dinner before she gives her talk?"

I was shaken by the look on Joni's face when we arrived, a look I hadn't seen since Shock Trauma days many years ago.

"What's happened, Jon?" I wrapped my arms around her neck, lingering, wanting to comfort, console, and, yes, rescue once again.

For an hour, she sobbed and poured out her heart. We listened in stunned silence.

Time to take the stage arrived too quickly. We dried Joni's tears and touched up her makeup. Through my own tears, I managed to say, "Oh, Jon, hang on. God is so faithful. Even this is from him for our good. I love you."

Joni rolled into the spotlight on the spacious stage. Several thousand boys erupted into applause. We huddled backstage in prayer as she began to speak. The Spirit of the living God filled her broken body and heart. And the auditorium.

Tom and I drove home contemplating what had happened. We were shaken by what Joni had privately shared with us. But even more, we were awed by witnessing God's strength being made perfect in her weakness as the audience was visibly moved by her message.

After that night I sensed the past had ended, and an unknown future had begun. This stirring scene at Hershey would repeat itself thousands of times in thousands of auditoriums around the globe in the decades that followed.

CHAPTER 24 — LEFT BEHIND

Catalog orders continued to pour in. Large duffel bags of mail continued to be answered. Administrative details continued to be addressed.

Unexpectedly, Judy called one day in March 1979. "Joni wants to come and talk to you and Tom."

"Sure." I replied.

I was surprised that Judy was in Sykesville, not California, and I was thankful we would be able to talk heart-to-heart and face-to-face without distractions.

Tom helped Judy transfer Joni out of the car and into the wheelchair. He lifted her chair up the single backdoor step and pushed her into the living room. Judy and Joni sat opposite Tom and me as the conversation began.

"Joni has decided to permanently move to California, and I will work with her to make that happen," said Judy.

"Is it necessary to move that far?" I asked.

"Yes," Joni replied.

No one ever considered she could or would move that far from her support systems. We were all wrong.

Joni's decision to move to California was fueled by regaining the ability to physically motor herself from point A to point B in the battery-powered wheelchair and gaining independence from an assortment of constraints. Judy had offered to oversee Joni's personal care, help relocate her permanently to California, and facilitate the August launch of a new nonprofit organization with a new name, Joni and Friends.

The unanticipated, though inevitable, had happened. A necessary ending for those in Sykesville and a necessary new beginning for Joni in California.

Shortly thereafter, a Joni Unlimited, Inc. and Joni PTL Ministries, Inc. dissolution meeting was attended by our trademark lawyer, Mr. Eareckson, Joni, Jay, Tom, and me. We sat at Jay's dining room table while terms of dissolution were reduced to a few final details and mop-up responsibilities which were left to Tom and me.

In my head, I knew that Joni was the central cog in a wheel whose spokes and supporting structures (like me) were replaceable. I had no choice but to believe God was leading her to California to build a new thing for his glory and ultimately her good. But all my heart could cry was *why, why, why?*

Why, God, did you call me to make such a commitment to join Joni in this remarkable journey only to suddenly nullify it twelve years later?

I called all the Joni Unlimited employees to our home to inform them of the dissolution of the print and greeting card company. I knew the absence of their daily banter and camaraderie and the void created by the dissolution of the ministry would linger with all of us for many years. We sat in a circle in our living room. The heavy burden of officially closing this chapter in our lives was left to me.

Still in shock, my words were smothered by grief as I said, "Several days ago, Joni informed me she is permanently moving to California. We are closing Joni Unlimited. I'm so sorry. We know God doesn't make mistakes even when every thought screams in disbelief."

I don't remember what happened after that.

It takes time to grieve losses, adjust to changes, and find your way. For me it was a bumpy, painful road to recovery that lasted longer than I could have anticipated. I was disoriented by yet another out-of-control whirlwind of spiraling complexity that exceeded my capacity to manage well.

I gradually willed myself to make time for reflection. I began to remember and reclaim God's promises:

> And we know that in all things God works for the good of those who love him, who have been called according to his purpose. (Rom. 8:28)
>
> Give thanks in all circumstances; for this is God's will for you in Christ Jesus. (1 Thess. 5:18)
>
> Let us hold unswervingly to the hope we profess, for he who promised is faithful. (Heb. 10:23)
>
> But we have this treasure in jars of clay to show that this all-surpassing power is from God and not from us. We are hard pressed on every side, but not crushed; perplexed, but not in despair; persecuted, but not abandoned; struck down, but not destroyed. (2 Cor. 4:7–9)

At the same time, knowing that healthy growth must also include time to feel anger and grieve, I gave myself permission to ask all the "why" questions and cry out to God. Once again, he had torn me away from the known and ushered me into the unknown. It seems this puzzling process has always been in his perfect plan for my life. I could not forget Jonah 2:8, "Those who cling to worthless idols turn away from God's love for them." As much as I hurt, I did not want to resist God's will for me and forfeit even a smidgeon of his unfailing promises and limitless grace. No idol of my own making was worth that.

Is this your way of faithfully pursuing me until you have my full attention? Until my will is firmly in the grip of your will and unconditional love?

PART 5

CHAPTER 25 — MOPPING UP THE MESS

Tom and I struggled through the task of undoing what we had worked for and accomplished with Joni. Dismantling wooden storage units and work benches. Packing up, selling, shipping, or giving away all that remained in the warehouse. World Wide Publications purchased, at cost, the remaining Joni prints and greeting cards, which enabled us to pay all outstanding invoices to our suppliers. Carol, the Joni Unlimited warehouse manager, helped with the grunt work until the place was empty. We were grateful for her emotional and practical support.

I organized and preserved paper remnants and hundreds of color slides and photos of the years with Joni in scrapbooks and meticulously stored them in archive boxes. I tucked them into a far corner of the attic where they remained unopened for four decades.

Tom continued to run the Village Gallery, now losing money as he was no longer framing matted prints ordered from the Joni Unlimited catalog. We lived on what remained of the liquidation funds for the next two years. Tom's emotional defenses were inadequate to cope with the stress and disruption we were facing. Feelings of humiliation and failure immobilized him, and he increasingly withdrew into himself. His chronic depression became disabling. He had little to give and barely functioned for months at a time.

I was intensely feeling the accumulated pain of eight years of Tom's emotional abuse, indifference, and rejection now that the ministry with Joni had ended. I, too, struggled with acute depression. Persistent colitis and abdominal cramping plagued my days. To add to the stress, I was frequently called upon any hour of the day or night to manage my mother's catatonic episodes and periods of uncontrollable rage, usually fueled by alcohol.

𝒟

I decided to share a deep desire with my husband on what seemed like a stress-free evening. Now might be a good time to hold out a little hope for our family's future. I was mistaken.

"Tom, I would like to have one more child. It would be so wonderful to have a little girl."

"Stop talking about having more children," he yelled back as he spun around and threw an armful of things across the room. "No! We can't get pregnant. I don't want any more children. I can't handle it. We can't afford it. You'll get even fatter. I don't want to talk about this again."

That was the end of my deep yearning for another child. *Oh, God. Not again. Rebuffed. Ugly. Unloved.*

I quietly retreated into the bathroom, locked the door, sank to the floor, stuffed a towel in my mouth, and cried for a long time.

One afternoon not long after that, Tom was on his knees installing new toe molding in our long hallway. The nails kept bending when the hammer's head struck. He cursed repeatedly as he raised his right arm high over his head and hammered our beautiful oak floor planks several times, leaving deep gouge marks in the wood. Afterward, when I passed that spot, I saw those dents, and new gouge marks dented my heart.

"Tom, why don't we pray together? It might be helpful," I offered one evening.

"Pray? No one is listening to my prayers. I don't believe that stuff anymore. Where is God when I need Him?"

Thankfully, these outbursts didn't last long, but they kept recurring. I watched his emotions build up steam like a pressure cooker, and then they'd erupt in cursing, followed by bouts of diarrhea.

He frightens me. Who was this man I married? I didn't know him at all. Perhaps I never had.

I frequently slipped away in the night to grieve and argue with God in secluded places. An ornate chapel at a nearby retreat center after midnight. The well-worn rear booth at Denny's diner in Sykesville where I hunched over cups of coffee until daybreak. Head resting on the steering wheel of my car in the moonlight beside the meandering Patapsco on a lonely bend in River Road.

This is too much, God. You promised I wouldn't be tempted with more than I could bear. I can't leave this marriage. Where's the escape hatch you promised?

CHAPTER 26—A HUSBAND'S BETRAYAL

One uneventful morning while volunteering at church, I was summoned to the phone to take a call from Tom.

"I need to tell you something," he said. "I have been fantasizing about my old girlfriend all these years. When I'm intimate with you, I'm visualizing her. I know it's wrong. I know I've hurt you. Please forgive me."

I said goodbye and collapsed on the office floor, doubled over in pain, crying, unable to speak. Sylvia, my good friend, heard me wailing and ran for Russ, a psychotherapist who worked at the church. Once I calmed down enough to speak, I didn't stop for an hour.

I finally understood the cause of Tom's rejection, shaming glances, and comments, but the way forward was no clearer to me. Questions collided in my mind: *How can I respond to this? Walk away like Mom? Forgive him? Eight years, so many tears, how could I forget? And why was he telling me now?*

"I can see your strength as you trust Jesus with everything. I thought you might be able to handle the truth now," Tom had said over the phone.

The truth Tom was expecting me to handle, however, was piled on top of a mountain of sorrows already weighing me down. Joni's move to California—the loss of friends, coworkers, and a fulfilling ministry—the potential of personal bankruptcy—the constant burden of Mom's ongoing problems—Dad's hurtful disinterest—and low self-esteem fueled by my husband's emotional withdrawal. I was overwhelmed and depressed.

I soothed my pain with food, gained weight and heaped more guilt and shame on myself. This generated more scornful looks and intolerable comments from Tom, and I soothed the fresh wounds with more food.

Sugar, my old friend, always made me immediately feel better, calmer. I would drive to Giant Food Store and head straight for the bakery case with the individual portions of my most pleasurable delights. *Let's see. Which one will help the most? There it is. The German chocolate cake with gobs of milk chocolate icing laced with flakes of coconut. Not too small, but not too large to be considered gluttonous.* I'd hurry to the express checkout and then straight to the car. Next step, to find a place to park where no one would see me shoveling down the cake.

As I kept eating, I complained out loud, "Why isn't this making me feel better?"

By 1980, at age thirty-one, I tipped the scale at 285. I railed against myself like the apostle Paul when he wrote, "What a wretched man I am! Who will rescue me from this body that is subject to death?" (Rom. 7:24).

Death by grieving, death by broken heart, death by obesity and relentless despair. Even sugar, this faithful old friend, couldn't soothe the pain cutting my heart into little pieces, shaving years off my life.

I felt discomfort in my chest. At times, my racing heart pounded so hard it rattled my skull. Was I having a heart attack? I was frightened enough to contact a cardiologist and begin my journey toward nonstop atrial fibrillation and a lifetime of medications to prevent a stroke.

CHAPTER 27 – FAITHFUL FRIENDS

God's Spirit cleansed and cauterized my weeping wounds through the loving words and caring deeds of others in the aftermath of Tom's devastating phone call about his old girlfriend.

Sylvia, a former pastor's wife, had been present immediately after Tom's phone call to hold my hand and listen and pray with me. She knew adversity and shattered dreams well and took the risk of being vulnerable with me. Her empathy produced comfort, and comfort produced emotional healing in the middle of the muck. She was often the bearer of tea and tenderness. This friendship is still precious today as we meet, chat, and pray for one another and our families.

Jessie, my sister, was also a compassionate listener. She had married Joe, a dentist, in 1979 and moved to Florida. She and her two small children occasionally returned to Maryland to visit Mom. Jessie and I shared each other's burdens and joys on those visits and during frequent phone calls. What a joy and precious gift to have such a wonderful, wise, and loving sister.

Cassie, my youngest sister, remained nearby. She was married in 1982, had one child, was divorced, and had remarried. Some of her choices led to hard times, financial problems, heartache, and multiple complications. We helped each other in good times and bad, and together we rescued Mom from recurring calamities in her declining years. Cassie got a BA degree in vocal performance, developed a beautiful coloratura soprano voice, and was an opera singer for many years. She also studied and developed exceptional typing and secretarial skills. She now lives in Florida near Jessie, and we fly back and forth for visits and special occasions.

Bonnie has been a best friend for fifty-seven years. We met as teens at Overcomers gatherings and became kindred spirits. She traveled with Joni and me to the Lincoln Center Art Exhibit in 1975, and Joni Unlimited introduced her colorful greeting cards in 1978. For decades, we traveled back and forth between Maryland and New Jersey for all of life's milestones—holidays, weddings, births, deaths, special occasions, or because we could. In my lowest seasons, Bonnie called me once a week, listened to hours of lament, and shared spiritual insights that had sustained her through her unmet longings for children, the sudden death of her mom, and the joy of adopting two children.

Eventually divorcing her first husband for infidelity, Bonnie married her high school sweetheart, who was a widowed pastor in a Bible Presbyterian church in Washington. Today, Bonnie paints at her watercolor table crowded with pencils, brushes, and trays. She surveys a wide northwest vista outside a big picture window framed with pine trees, bird houses, and flowerpots, with Mt. Rainier in the distance. She often calls while painting, and we chat for hours. We always end with "Love you." What a blessing she is to me!

Cousin Rachel, two years younger than I, lives in Pennsylvania, and I see her most often. After she married Ed Hardesty, they moved to Texas where he graduated from Dallas Seminary and eventually returned to Maryland to pastor a church. Dr. Hardesty, now retired, was a Hebrew Studies professor at Cairn University near Philadelphia. This couple is very dear to me. Humble, wise, faithful servants, exemplary parents and grandparents, who sacrificed everything and achieved more. Both have supported me in every way.

These are a few of God's followers who love me unconditionally and are instruments of enduring healing, ministering to my sorrows, and helping me get up and keep going after each knockdown.

$$\mathscr{D}$$

By 1980, Liberty Reformed Presbyterian Church had decided to start a Christian school on their spacious property. The church also offered an interesting Sunday school class on Reformed theology that I eagerly attended. I first met Terry in that class. She and her family had recently become members, and the pastor had asked her to be on the new school board as personnel chairman.

Starting a new private school was challenging, and personnel was a big start-up issue. Terry needed a personnel assistant, and she had heard about my business and administrative experience from my friend, Sylvia. When the board chairman approached me to become assistant personnel chairman, I agreed and soon discovered this new challenge was helping to restore my sense of self-esteem and purpose.

Terry and I became good friends while working on the personnel committee from 1981 to 1985. We shared a passion for ministry, a vision for God's purposes, and a commitment to following in his steps. *Here we are, Lord, send us.* We were privileged to help launch the school, which still provides a quality Christian education to children.

Young Life was also near and dear to our hearts, and Howard County Young Life needed new committee chairmen to oversee ministry policy and procedures. Terry and I jumped in with four feet from 1986 to 1990 since our children attended local club activities. We chaired monthly meetings, visited Saranac Lake Summer Camp in upstate New York, and worked to make the annual fundraising banquet a big success.

In December 1986, Terry was diagnosed with breast cancer and, a month later, had the first of two mastectomies that year with nine rounds of chemotherapy sandwiched in between. Both her daughters, still in high school, rallied around emotionally, but they also needed to stay focused on their studies. Her husband was busy in his demanding career. Help was needed to fill in the gaps during her surgeries and chemo treatments at Johns Hopkins Hospital.

I knew how to do this. I had lots of practical experience. That's what friends are for. Praying as the gurney rolled into the surgical suite, holding her hand when painful procedures were performed, and holding the trashcan to catch vomit when the chemo kicked in—I could do that, and I did. I read Scripture to her to pass the time during lengthy chemo infusions and prayed with her when fear and anxiety invaded her thoughts. We grew to know each other well during this time. Passing through dark valleys of pain and fear does that when you love a friend with the same love Christ pours out on you.

The reverse happened when I had an acute gall bladder attack on June 12, 1992. I was doubled over in pain as the ambulance rushed me to St. Agnes Hospital, where the nearly gangrenous and gallstone-filled body part was laparoscopically removed. I recuperated at home for a week or two, and Terry played nurse.

Other opportunities to serve each other followed over time. In addition, Terry and I spent hours eagerly digging into Bible passages, searching for new insights into lingering problems and challenges we each faced.

As had happened with other people God brought into my life, Terry and I were living out a friendship principle King Solomon wrote down long ago:

> Two are better than one, because they have a good return for their labor: If either of them falls down, one can help the other up. But pity anyone who falls and has no one to help them up. (Eccles. 4:9–10)

CHAPTER 28—REPAIRING THE BREACH

Another friend was continually on my mind amid the marriage and family turmoil. My world had been tossed upside down after Joni unexpectedly left Sykesville to move to Los Angeles. A long season of grieving and uncertainty set in. The loss of a friend, the loss of ministry, the loss of vision and dreaming big dreams were hard valleys to journey through. I likened it to a type of sudden death experience, as Joni and I lost contact with each other for a while.

But God spoke to my heart about Joni. When God's Spirit speaks into a receptive heart, torn fragments of painful memories begin to mend, and gaping wounds begin to heal. The good news of the gospel of Jesus Christ is the only force in the universe that reconciles us to God and each other.

In the fall of 1982, the gospel aroused dormant emotions in me, and the following is an excerpt from a letter I wrote to Joni:

> No matter how much time passes or how diligently I try to blot the past from my thoughts, one thing becomes clearer: my love for you is greater than the sadness I still feel. Painful scenes obstinately replay in my mind when my memory is jogged. Sometimes I still cry after recalling a happy time or place. I don't have any answers or suggestions. No insights

or words of wisdom. No inspirational phrases. I realized how foolish it was not to say at least these few words if nothing else.

Reconstructing the past is futile, I think. I question what the future holds, given the physical distance and the different paths our lives have taken. There's not much common ground between us anymore.

What can we do to bridge the distance between us.

Love, Diana

Joni had met Ken Tada in 1981 at John MacArthur's church in Sun Valley, California. After her engagement to Ken, she came back to Baltimore to introduce him to extended family and friends. They stopped by our home for a short visit. The gals planning Joni's bridal shower in California had contacted me to submit a square for a large quilt they were making as a collective gift from many old and new friends. I was pleased to be asked, but what would it say or depict? I mulled over this question for weeks and finally decided it should depict an open Bible with "A friend loves at all times" (Prov. 17:17), written boldly over its open pages. Since I didn't sew, I asked Terry to make it for me.

I received an invitation to the rehearsal dinner and attended the wedding on July 3, 1982. I invited Terry to go with me as my guest. The night before the wedding, I unexpectedly had a good cry. Terry was a great comforter as I released pent-up emotions. The wedding was a beautiful, joyous celebration of love and commitment, and I was happy to be there despite all the unspoken questions in my heart and soul. It represented a small beginning in rebuilding the foundations of my friendship with Joni and hers with me.

Six months after their wedding, I got a call that Joni and Ken were on a short East Coast visit and had a few hours of free time. I invited them to dinner, and they came. We had a lovely evening together. I showed Ken the two large scrapbooks I had compiled of our ministry together. He was amazed.

Joni's letters continued sporadically through the 80s and 90s. Warm, cordial, encouraging, full of new travels, events, art projects, and occasionally, distant memories of happy times. I enjoyed reading each letter and praised God for all he was accomplishing.

In April 2007, the Joni and Friends International Disability Center ceremoniously opened with ribbon-cutting, picture-taking, a reception for all the guests, tours, singing, and lots of joy. Terry and I flew out to join the celebrations. Steve Estes and his wife, Verna, were also there along with other old and new friends. This was the culmination of all that had happened in the previous forty years since Joni broke her neck.

Before leaving for California, I decided it was time to open the old Joni Unlimited boxes covered with forty years of undisturbed dust. I had painfully packed up all the miscellaneous papers, catalogs, and records from the warehouse and tucked them away deep in the attic rafters. I didn't anticipate how sad I would be as I sorted through boxes of archives from those years. Among other items, I found the old black music stand with an adjustable tray I first got her for reading books by herself.

I decided to give Joni both oversized, leather scrapbooks I had made, filled with memorabilia—letters, photos, articles, brochures, schedules, plane ticket stubs, fliers, and more. They contained an accurate record of our early years together—1967 to 1979. This chronological history of Joni's and my past years together abruptly stopped in October 1979. Although the contents were truly *ours*, they were *hers* to have. I copied what I wanted and mailed the rest to her.

A year later in July 2008, I received a letter in the mail from her.

> Next year is the thirtieth anniversary of Joni
> and Friends, and we are hoping to put together

a photo book of the history of the ministry—some of those photos we will pull from the scanned archive books. Thank you again for all the hard work you invested in this project so many years ago. Who would have thought that it would have helped lay the foundation for so much ministry around the world. I'm humbled, as I know you are, too. May every blessing of Ruth 2:12 be yours!

I looked up the verse Joni noted in her letter: "May the Lord repay you for what you have done. May you be richly rewarded by the Lord, the God of Israel, under whose wings you have come to take refuge" (Ruth 2:12).

In 2009, I received a twelve-by-twelve-inch package from Joni and Friends in the mail. To my complete surprise, I unwrapped a hundred-page book full of color photographs and items from the two scrapbooks I had given her the previous year. Happy tears flowed.

Lord, I still have many unanswered questions about what happened before, during, and after those years. But I know, without a doubt, that "in all things God works for the good of those who love him, who have been called according to his purpose" (Rom. 8:28).

Thank you for unconditionally loving me through the intervening years. Please continue to teach me to lay down my human dreams and take up your good and perfect plans for me and my family, whatever they may be. All things are in your hands. Who can I trust but you?

CHAPTER 29 – PARENTING THE BOYS

Alienation in the bedroom, Tom's chronic depression, and our continuous financial problems were not going to prevent me from being the best mom possible. My heart was full of love for my sons. I used every ounce of energy to focus on them and protect them from the relentless calamity that took up residence in our home and lives. Andy sensed it all. Michael was easily distracted and self-oriented, but still he knew.

When not hindered by depression, Tom engaged in teaching the boys skills: how to operate, use, make, build, and fix things. He was particularly good at that.

We had built a beautiful home with lots of space to grow. We had wide, gently sloping grassy areas for all sorts of games and activities and two rough-and-tumble wooded acres for dirt bike, go-cart, and motorcycle trails. It was an idyllic setting with sandboxes, swings, climbers, campfires, gardens, half-pipe ramps for skateboarding, above-ground swimming pools, and a menagerie of critters, large and small.

We had joined Liberty Reformed Presbyterian Church shortly after we were married in 1971. Rev. Mark Pett was young, gifted, and very personable. Our family attended Sunday school and church, but as the boys got older, Tom only went occasionally.

Andy entered preschool and then kindergarten at Calvary Baptist School, and he thrived. We stretched our meager finances like a tight rubber band to pay the tuition. Tom's old Barracuda and my hatchback Maverick limped along thanks to his tinkering. Andy remained at Calvary Baptist through elementary school, then transferred to a public middle school closer to home. He wanted to stay at Calvary, but we could no longer afford the tuition. Andy graduated from high school in 1992.

Michael stayed with me while a toddler. I set up elaborate play stations in and outside the house. When he turned three, we enrolled him in Liberty's preschool. He loved it. He was an extrovert and thrived on being with friends. After sixth grade we transferred him to public school, a necessary financial decision but painful.

We saved money for a three-week tent camping trip to the Rockies and back, northern and southern routes. Two years later, we took a trip to Disney World and Cape Canaveral.

Howard County General Hospital got to know us well with Andy's assorted broken bones and Michael's emergency appendectomy and concussions from bike and skateboard mishaps. Broken, chipped, and displaced teeth kept the dental surgeons busy.

Sunday school and church; private art, music, and swimming lessons; and community team sports crowded our days year-round. We spent countless hours at baseball, basketball, and soccer practices and games; swimming lessons at the YMCA, school performances, and awards ceremonies. Andy became a star soccer player, tending the goal on community league teams through the high school varsity team as a freshman. He was captain and center linebacker on the high school football team.

We provided meaningful opportunities that our limited resources allowed to give them the best possible memories, training, and spiritual foundations for happy successful lives. We wanted to make their childhoods better than ours.

Still, we were flawed role models as a couple and as parents. I showered hugs and "I love yous" on each of the boys, but none were exchanged between Tom and me. I believe this eventually contributed to a lack of confidence in the boys' relational skills with girls and later, with the women they dated. Unintended consequences lingered into adulthood and may have strained their ability to be the spouses and role models God fully intended them to become.

CHAPTER 30—MEANWHILE, MOTHER

Mom's affair with Hank, which started when I was still in middle school, was predictably tumultuous. Still, she had married him in 1974. They sold the house in Lochearn and moved to Eldersburg, closer to me. Jessie and Cassie remained with them. They were seventeen and fifteen.

Why was Mom addicted to this toxic relationship? I suppose Hank was the Hollywood, debonair, romantic type she idolized as a teen. Not all that handsome, he could be a charmer, but underneath he was a con artist.

Hank was late coming home from work one evening soon after they married. Jessie and Cassie weren't home. I was there and witnessed what happened.

Mom was fuming after one too many drinks, suspecting something was wrong.

"I'm going to catch him this time," her slurred words announced as she slammed the heavy door of her Lincoln Continental and sped off. I tried to stop the unstoppable but failed and followed in hot pursuit. She stopped at a red light. Ahead of us was Hank's Lincoln, parked next to a glass-enclosed payphone on the next corner.

When the light turned green, Mom floored the accelerator, sped across the street and turned her ramrod into the parking lot. She violently slammed into the booth, twice, with Hank in it, until it lay sideways on the asphalt. Backing up quickly, then turning the car around, she sped back across the intersection and passed me.

Hank pried his way out of the twisted metal, brushed the glass off himself, and got into his car. Satisfied he was still alive and appeared to be uninjured, I followed Mom back home to make certain she arrived safely, but I didn't go in. I had witnessed enough and didn't want to see more. I prayed all the way home that they wouldn't kill each other if he returned that night.

$$\mathcal{D}$$

On another occasion, my phone rang at two in the morning.

"Diana? You've got to come over now," Hank shouted. "It's your mother. You've got to come immediately."

"OK. I'll be there in fifteen minutes." I sped through pitch-black, deserted country roads to their house.

"She's in the closet. Curled up on the floor. Incoherent."

Lord, help me. I'm so angry. She's made such a mess of her life. I've had enough. Make her stop.

Apparently, they had been arguing. Hank decided to frighten her by pretending to shoot himself in the head and falling to the floor, feigning death. Mom went berserk, had a psychotic break with reality, and curled up in a fetal position in the bedroom closet.

"Mom. Get up. Mom? Hank's not dead. Look. He's right here. Mom? Mom? He's not dead. Look."

I was ready to call an ambulance when she roused from her mental breakdown. Hank and I helped her over to the bed where she collapsed and went to sleep.

Mercifully, my memory has erased all other details of that frightful night.

D

My sisters' wedding stories give additional glimpses into life with our mother.

Jessie's Wedding Dress Story: "It was July 1979. My wedding to Joe was rapidly approaching. The bright morning sunlight embraced the part of my face that wasn't covered by bedsheets. My thoughts focused on one thing—my wedding dress. What did I want? Would I find something I liked? Couldn't be too expensive. What mood would Mom be in this morning? Oh, Lord, please, I want this day to go well. Please.

Get up, get dressed, don't forget the bridal magazine with my favorites earmarked.

Mom was screaming and raging throughout the house. Had she started drinking already? It was so early. My dreams for this special day plummeted into another terrifying nightmare with Mom.

An anonymous phone caller had revealed that Hank, her second husband for whom she had practically and emotionally abandoned all else, including me, had been cheating on her with another woman the whole time he was with her. Explosive anger continually erupted during the drive to the bridal shop, the dress try-ons, the fitting, and the ride home.

I couldn't wait to get out of this house."

Cassie's Wedding Day Story: "It was June 5, 1982. So far, so good. The wedding photographer had arrived on time at Mom's house to photograph me and my bridesmaids, Di, Jessie, and Cousin Rachel. When finished with photos, we would step into a limousine for the thirty-minute drive to North Point Baptist Church.

Without any warning, ear-piercing shrieking, screaming, and cursing enveloped the whole house. Di ran down the hallway toward the sound to find Mom locked in the bathroom, wailing uncontrollably.

'What's the matter?' Di yelled twisting the resistant

doorknob. 'Open the door,' she insisted. 'Open the door.'

Mom was pounding on the wall with her fists, still screaming.

'Open the door. Let me in!' Di repeated.

The door swung open. Amid the crying, Mom showed Di that the zipper on the back of her dress would not close. She was consumed by a raging panic attack because her dress no longer fit, and she couldn't fix it no matter how forcefully she yanked and pulled.

'Take it off,' Di yelled. 'Take it off. The seamstress is not far away. She'll let out the seams and zipper margins. We'll make it work. Calm down and give it to me.'

She turned to her husband—'Tom, quick, take this down the street to the seamstress and give her this note with instructions.'

Mom continued to rail and moan as she retreated to her bedroom. Di, Jessie, Cousin Rachel, and I tried to pull ourselves together for the photographer. Then Michael, Di's mischievous youngest, accidentally stepped on my full-skirted dress and a long gaping tear opened on the back. Now I was yelling.

Terry, Di's friend, swung into action. She crawled under my dress with needle and thread in hand and mended the tear as the photographer took photos.

Thirty minutes later, Tom returned with Mom's dress that had been let out and reinforced as much as possible. Miraculously, the zipper closed. Mom's panicky emotions calmed down, and off we went to the church."

This sort of mayhem continued off and on for years. I would be called to intervene during one altercation after another. It all ended when Hank had a fatal heart attack in August 1991, having refused to go to the hospital when he first noticed uncomfortable chest pains days before. We never understood why he wouldn't go to the hospital until several days after his death when a coworker brought Hank's briefcase to Mom. Inside were multiple years of neatly stacked pay stubs, chronicling hundred-dollar treasury bonds automatically deducted from his paychecks and deposited into another woman's checking account. He didn't want a long stay in the hospital because his paycheck would be mailed to the house for Mom to discover his secret.

CHAPTER 31—DAD'S LEGACY

When Dad was living with us in Sykesville, he decided to date Lizzy, a single woman he knew from a piano store in Gaithersburg.

In May 1975, he announced, "I'm going to marry Lizzy next month."

"Please repeat after me … ," the pastor said.

"I, John, take thee, Elizabeth, to be my wedded wife," my father repeated.

Unexpectedly, I burst into uncontrollable tears and loud sobbing while trapped in the middle of a long pew at Stone Chapel, sitting next to Tom and my sisters,. I covered my mouth with a handful of tissues, leaned forward to hide my face, and wept through the entire ceremony. Decades of suppressed emotion could no longer be contained. When grief grabs you by the throat and won't let go, you've no choice but to release it.

It turned out, though, that Dad and Lizzy were a good match, both odd around the margins but seemingly happy enough. She was a penny pincher and wanted financial security. He was peculiar and wanted no debts. Neither seemed interested in quality time with my family or my sisters' families. We rarely saw them in the intervening years except for Easter, Thanksgiving, and Christmas dinners.

D

Dad called one day early in November 1996. "My doctor incorrectly diagnosed me with type 2 diabetes a year ago, as you already know. Pancreatic cancer has now been confirmed as the real problem, and I am having surgery next week."

"Oh, Dad, I'm so sorry. When and where is your surgery? We'll be there."

A week later, while he was in recovery after two hours of abdominal surgery, the surgeon came out to speak with the family. Lizzy, Tom, Jessie, Cassie, and I were there.

"We removed the suspicious tissue, but the cancer is so advanced throughout his abdomen, organs, and connective ducts that nothing else can be done. We sutured him up. We recommend appropriate chemo to try to prolong his life as long as possible."

"How much time?" I asked.

"Six months at best," he replied.

"How much extra time will the chemo give him?" I continued to probe.

"Two weeks, give or take a few days."

"Then why make his last eight months miserable with chemo side effects?" I continued.

"There's a lot we don't know. We can learn a lot by giving him these new drug protocols if your father agrees."

I had heard enough. What about quality of life in his final months? Why not deal with the pain as it comes and let him remain as active as possible? I was angry. But Dad wanted to try the chemo. To this day, I believe they misled him into believing it would appreciably prolong his life. He was relatively young at seventy and was content living at a nice retirement community in Baltimore. He was servicing his customers and tuning their pianos daily. He loved his work.

It quickly became clear, however, that he was unable to work due to the sickening side effects of the chemo cocktails. He rapidly declined, losing weight, unable to eat, eventually unable to walk.

By July, during Dad's final weeks, he and I had several talks alone. He told me he had established a trust for Jessie, Cassie, and me several years earlier. He had been saving his income for years investing in many different stocks, bonds, annuities, and CDs. His investments had grown beyond his expectations, and he hoped to leave a significant inheritance for each of us.

I had one final conversation with Dad before he mentally slipped away.

"Diana, have I been a good father?" he asked, frail and weak, seated across from me at his dining room table. He was struggling to sit upright, to look the part of the strong, loving father he had tried his best to be, to communicate how he loved me in the only way he knew.

I saw faint glimpses of hope in his eyes, searching for a word of love and affirmation from me, as his life ebbed away. Before this moment he had never asked this of me. He'd never asked my forgiveness for his brief lapse in self-control that had driven me out of the house many years ago. He had faithfully put up with Mom's anger and frustrations for years. He worked hard to provide things he believed his daughters needed that his earnings could provide. A college education that would give us the start in life he never had, but always desired. And now, a generous legacy for our senior years. Even though he was never comfortable saying it or never knew how, I sensed he was asking "Do you know how much I love you?"

I tried to quickly gather my thoughts and control my emotions as I quietly considered my response. In one question, his lifelong unspoken love was seeking affirmation. I could not deny his request. *Jesus, infuse me with love for my Dad. Fill me with your love for him and his love for me. Enable me to give him this final earthly gift of his daughter's love, respect, affirmation, and thankfulness that he longs for.*

Compassion led me to his side and forgiveness prevailed as I tearfully gave him a hug.

"Yes, Dad. You have been a good father. I love you."

The next day, Jessie arrived for what would be his final three weeks of life. Together, we had one final conversation with him.

"Dad, why did you make the trust revocable? Doesn't that mean Lizzy is able to change it?" we asked.

"I trust her. I wanted to make certain she has what she needs, and what remains at her passing will be yours. Don't forget about Lizzy when I'm gone."

He seemed to slip away after that. At his bedside we softly recited familiar verses from Psalm 23: "The Lord is my shepherd, I lack nothing ... Even though I walk through the darkest valley, I will fear no evil ...". At that moment, with eyes closed and body motionless, he joined us from memory finishing the psalm—"Surely your goodness and love will follow me all the days of my life, and I will dwell in the house of the Lord forever."

We helped him get comfortable on the bed which hospice had provided. He gradually slipped into semi-consciousness, and we cared for him, along with Lizzy, in their apartment until his passing.

Several days after his memorial service, Lizzy handed me three of Dad's things.

First, a card that had been sitting on Dad's office desk ever since she married him. It was in the shape of a grand piano with the top open, tattered around the edges, faded, and taped together in several places. Red hearts, dancing on a ribbon of musical score, depicted notes rising from the strings. If sung, they would sound like "Happy Birthday to You." Inside it said, "I love you, Dad. Diana." I had given it to him twenty-five years earlier, and he had kept it in view all those years.

Second, the wedding band Mom had placed on his finger on their wedding day. Today, I wear it on my right ring finger, to remember and honor Dad's legacy.

Third, the folded US flag that had draped his casket until it was lowered into the burial plot. Now, it's in a three-cornered display case sitting on my bedroom bookcase.

A good person leaves an inheritance for their children's children. (Prov. 13:22)

When Dad passed away, I asked the Lord this question. *What do you want me to learn from my father?* Nineteen years later, I discovered several answers to that question.

Many unknowns about my father remain. He didn't know how to be known, nor did he give any hints that he wanted or needed to be known. As a child he lacked emotional connections with his parents, siblings, and friends. Throughout life he seemed clueless about what to do when warm emotions were expected or required.

I saw tears in Dad's eyes at Dr. Slaght's funeral as he stood over his open casket and sang "Open the Gates of the Temple." [1] He loved and was loved by Arthur Slaght, who mentored, encouraged, and inspired him to be a man of good character. They were like father and adopted son.

I witnessed a warm and happy glow about him as he gave piggyback rides to Jessie and Cassie when they were toddlers. His gentle smile seemed to embrace them when his arms wouldn't, as he tucked them into their beds. It was a heartfelt expression of nonverbal love which was the most he could openly express. It was both touching and sad. All three of us desperately needed his more tangible affection and affirmations, but he was unable to give them in ways we could feel or remember as children or adults.

In 2016 after Lizzy's passing, my sisters and I discovered how faithfully Dad had worked and saved to leave an inheritance far greater than we could have imagined. Clearly this was evidence of the love my father could not express any other way. I feel loved by my earthly father. I love him for sacrificially taking care of us in the face of great adversity. For urging and enabling us to get an education and paying for it. For slipping us money, out of Lizzy's view, at Christmas, on birthdays, or when any of his daughters or grandchildren had unexpected needs, emergencies, or promising opportunities. For planning ahead, for creating a trust, for being a man of integrity, for being my dad. In heaven I want to give and receive all the hugs we missed.

What did I learn from my father?

To be a person of integrity. To be honest and ethical, always. To value education and never stop learning. To be responsible in all things. To make a commitment and keep it. To always speak the truth. To accept God's unfailing love.

CHAPTER 32—TAKING MYSELF IN HAND

Not long after I first met Terry at church, she suggested Tom and I make an appointment with Dr. Doris Morgan, a well-known Christian psychologist who had been an acquaintance of mine for years. We saw Doris once a week for two years. More secrets were uncovered, but real solutions were never attempted. Leaving her office after our final appointment together, Tom turned and said to Doris, "I thought you were going to fix her. Nothing has changed."

He was wrong. I was changing. He wasn't.

I continued psychotherapy sessions with Doris even after marital therapy ended. She handed me *Telling Yourself the Truth* by William Backus and Marie Chapian.[1]

On one occasion, I had to draw a picture of how I felt. I drew a woman, alone, in a chair, her whole body bound with rope and her mouth stuffed with rags. Eyes closed, tears running down her face, soaking the floor.

Later I brought in childhood photos, and Doris asked what I was feeling in each one.

My life had been tightly bound by others' pain. I had lost myself in their messes, while heaping more pain on myself. I never considered trying to rescue myself. I was too bound up in my own dysfunction to uncover deeper awareness without help.

With Doris's help, the putrid emotional bindings unwound, and I rediscovered that God loved me with an everlasting love. I relearned how to love and accept myself. I didn't need to be or do anything to earn that love.

The words from an old Charles Wesley hymn we sang at Young Life club years ago broke through my fog:

> Long my imprisoned spirit lay
> Fast bound in sin and nature's night;
> Thine eye diffused a quick'ning ray,
> I woke, the dungeon flamed with light;
> My chains fell off, my heart was free,
> I rose, went forth, and followed Thee.[2]

I didn't need Tom's love or acceptance, or anyone else's, to be at peace with myself. I already had peace with God.

By 1990, after nine years of economic ups and downs, Tom was forced to sell his second try at owning and operating a custom-designed and manufactured home and office furniture business. He descended into another depression-fueled season of dysfunction, more debilitating than the first, and continued to refuse to get help or medication. He tried various get-rich-quick, and multi-level-marketing schemes, then finally found employment designing and selling kitchens. He kept switching from company to company as they either failed or struggled in the gyrating housing market. Each change reset his salary at minimum wage.

I made the difficult decision not to seek full-time employment for two reasons. First, the boys needed me at home. Second, if I became the primary wage earner, I feared Tom would become comfortable letting me assume the responsibility of financially supporting the family. I found creative ways to generate additional income through self-employment projects.

I continued my full-court-press to resuscitate our marriage.

I assumed love could be rekindled, if I lost enough weight, was more available, initiated sex more frequently, forgave Tom more earnestly, gave him more respect, waited for him to take the lead, prayed for him more, found a mentor willing to invest in him, sought help from his family, encouraged him more, and on and on.

I read books, listened to audio tapes, and attended seminars too numerous to mention.

I found a local cognitive behavioral therapist who taught me to change my relationship to food. I lost forty pounds.

Tom and I took a personality profile inventory, and discovered we were extreme opposites. I explored how to cope with and appreciate the differences.

I wanted more education in a field that would give me valuable tools and healthier insights into people, ministry, and serving others. In 1986, I enrolled in night school at Loyola College, in Baltimore City, to study human behavior. I guzzled the required courses by reading thick textbooks, listening to experienced professors, and digging into research across the spectrum of disorders, therapies, and theories. I completed an internship with Doris at her local Christian counseling center practice. After four years of part-time, postgraduate night school, I received an MA in Counseling and Psychotherapy.

I examined each new insight and theory through the lens of biblical principles and discovered many fascinating things. The Bible is full of psychological principles which have been codified and affirmed by secular contemporary thinkers, practitioners, and research. They exploded off the pages as I reread the Bible and plumbed its wealth of psychological and emotional content. But the same secular experts had gone off the rails regarding other biblical truth. It was challenging and exciting to examine what I was learning under both microscopes, secular and sacred, to affirm truth and discard error.

After graduation in 1990, I saw private clients for three years at two counseling centers in Baltimore County.

I spent ten years growing spiritually and changing my unhealthy behavioral patterns. I put hours of concentrated effort into becoming more aware, accepting personal responsibility, maintaining a clear conscience, breaking free of codependency, developing healthy boundaries, attempting to restore intimacy, working on forgiveness, setting realistic expectations, and being more compassionate in adversity.

All this failed to bring reconciliation in our marriage.

But our marriage was not only about me—it was also about Tom. I had opened the secret closets of my life and invited the Holy Spirit to clean house, every corner. The marriage could not be saved unless Tom was willing to do the same. He wasn't able or willing.

I slammed into helplessness and railed against it.

CHAPTER 33—NO MORE SEX

Tom and I weren't having sex very often since his confession about an old sweetheart. One night after fifteen or twenty minutes of effort, Tom unemotionally stated, "I can't do this anymore." And that was that. After nineteen years of marriage, only a legal and financial arrangement remained. Ironically, I was relieved at not having to endure more of the same.

It was August 1990. I was forty-one. Half my life was behind me. My mother had secretly committed adultery for ten years and had finally gotten a divorce. My father, with biblically sanctioned reasons for divorce, married again, resulting in unexpected consequences after his passing. What would I do about my crumbling marriage?

I could choose martyrdom by remaining in a hopelessly dead, emotionally abusive relationship, sacrificing happiness in this life for the next, and perilously clinging to the promises of no more tears and joys forevermore beyond the grave.

I could accept celibate separation, denying myself the joys of intimacy in marriage yet preserving my marriage vows.

I could pursue intimacy with God who satisfies our deepest longings. *But how does that work, really?*

I could even choose tantalizing titillations through viewing pornography. *Can't be that bad. No one gets hurt, right? Not!*

I could choose denial, repressing truth to avoid reality, staying busy with good deeds, seeking purpose in the pain. Accumulating points to gain entry into heaven. *But it doesn't work that way, does it!*

I could even beg for natural death for myself or my spouse as release from rejection's intolerable loneliness.

Or I could acknowledge reality with one hand while grasping for God-honoring purpose and meaning with the other, teetering on the thin edge of a life worth living, praying for strength to persevere.

This is the path I choose, Lord. I don't want to repeat my mother's mistakes. No adultery. No legal separation. No divorce. If my marriage will end, it will not be by my doing.

This self-imposed solitary confinement locked me into more decades of hidden and sustained brokenness filled with rejection, loneliness, absence of physical intimacy, financial calamities, shattered dreams, weight gain, medical problems, and more. Yet, day by day as the Holy Spirit continued cleaning my internal closets, intimacy with Christ increased, and I found that purpose and meaning gradually filled the empty spaces.

CHAPTER 34 – ON MISSION

Long ago at an Overcomers summer camp, I was seated on a fallen log as smoke and red-hot embers rose from a twilight campfire. Surrounded by friends, with head bowed and hands raised, I embraced God's call to serve him with my whole self.

Here I am, Lord, send me.

Along the way, life happened. Dreams shattered. Plans crumbled. Losses multiplied. Illness taunted. Death called. My mind, emotions, and body were relentlessly pummeled, eventually causing more emotional trauma and physical maladies.

My spirit learned to persevere with every passing challenge as it desperately clung to God's promises and the certainty of his providence. Under the watchful care of faithful friends, old and new, I risked reengaging in meaningful activities.

As a member of Liberty Reformed Presbyterian Church, I decided to join the adult choir. Singing is a special medicine for the soul. Our family attended holiday church picnics, bonded at picnic tables, bantered on baseball fields, shared casseroles, and vied for the most sought-after desert.

Terry, her husband and two daughters, invited our struggling family to outings at local state parks for tent camping weekends. We bought tents, Coleman stoves and lanterns, sleeping bags, a canoe and other equipment. We hiked, canoed, roasted hotdogs and hamburgers on the grill and blackened marshmallows on long twigs over crackling campfires. Together, we took a three-week road trip to the continental divide in our vans, tent camping every night at different National Parks. We visited the Badlands, Jackson Hole, Yellowstone, Grand Tetons, Bryce Canyon, Zion, Gunnison, Mesa Verde, Great Smokies, and Shenandoah.

Maybe there was hope for Tom and me and the boys.

Entering the 1990s, I still had many unanswered questions. But I knew who was in control, and it wasn't me. Self was slowly dying, and the Holy Spirit filled those vacant spaces with himself. As my grip on self-control loosened, God's grip on me increased.

Liberty Church had started a new Christian school and asked Terry and me to join the school board as volunteer co-chairmen of personnel. During our five-year commitment, the school grew and prospered. It then became clear that God was directing us elsewhere.

We were apostolic, creative developers, visionary women who identified and sought out underserved problems and populations with our problem-solving skills and passionate commitment to make an impact. We recruited others to the vision, trained and equipped future leaders, supervised the project development for the initial five years, and then transferred the initiative to others more inclined to maintain and grow the vision. Multiplying and replacing ourselves was the goal, not running in place. What did God have in mind for us next?

We joined a Young Life team on a trip to the former Soviet Union where nonviolent political and social transformations were taking place. A new era of religious freedom and hunger to learn about Christianity made it a strategic time to explore potential ministries for teenagers. This was my first trip outside the United States. I was finally a missionary—in Russia of all places! For two weeks anyway.

Terry and I retreated and prayed upon our return, asking God for wisdom and direction. Our desire was to serve a ministry as part-time volunteers, remain at home, and parent our children through their teenage years. They would soon be off to college and independent lives.

With our mission pastor's encouragement, we flew to Phoenix, Arizona, with a team from our church, to learn about the CoMission. It was a new initiative formed by eighty ministry groups to take the message of Christ's love to the Russian people. We met, worked with, and were trained by gifted leaders from many esteemed parachurch organizations who had committed their organizations and resources toward making a big dream a reality. And they did.

The Navigators, a parachurch organization, bent their customary staff recruitment protocol and immediately embraced us as vision casters and communication specialists and loaned us to work with the CoMission headquarters team. CoMission recruited thousands of lay people to spend a year in Russia and teach basic Christianity to public school teachers so they could teach it to their students across eleven time zones.

It was a great privilege to hear, learn from, and work with many illustrious Christian statesmen and women. We learned about humility, networking, collaboration, sharing resources, developing a cooperative plan, and implementing that plan with great impact over that five-year period. The lessons we learned have inspired and shaped all we have done since.

Terry and I joined the Navigator Community entity when CoMission ended in 1997, and looked for a new, underserved population to focus on. By 1998, we determined that church-based ESL programs were greatly needed in Maryland. We got ourselves up to speed teaching ESL, recruited and trained a team of volunteers from our home church, and launched our first ESL program in 1998.

I'm not sure what Terry and I expected from the ESL ministry, but it wasn't the drama that unfolded on an early morning phone call.

"I can't do it. I can't do it!" was all I understood as a new Korean-American ESL student spoke through sobs.

"Joy, may I come over to your townhouse right now? I can't understand what you're saying."

"Yes. Please come now," she replied.

"Oh, Diana," was all I understood in the flood of garbled words that greeted me as Joy opened the door, and I reached out to embrace her. Seated at the kitchen table, she drew in deep breaths as her moaning subsided.

"What is happening, Joy?" I asked.

For the next two hours Joy emptied her grieving soul as she shared that she and her husband, Samuel, had decided they had no choice but to abort her third pregnancy.

They had no relatives or close friends in the United States who could help her through nine months of extreme prenatal nausea and complications that often required frequent hospitalizations for rehydration and exhaustion. Samuel had to work long hours every day, and it would be impossible for her to care for herself and their two small children alone. This decision violated their conscience and belief in God-given human life at conception, but they concluded they had no alternative.

God, help Joy and Samuel. Help us. What can we say or do?

"Joy, God loves you and your family. He has created this life in your womb. He will make a way for you to have this child. Please wait for forty-eight hours before you take any irreversible actions. I will share this with Terry, and we will make a few phone calls. Let's see what God will do."

Her tiny self wrapped both arms around my considerably larger shoulders as she nestled her tear-soaked face next to mine.

"Thank you, Diana. I will wait for your phone call."

Terry and I contacted all the volunteer teachers and assistants in our church's conversational ESL program, explaining the urgent needs of this family, and asking for their help. Without hesitation, thirty ladies committed themselves to collectively love these neighbors as themselves.

Two days later, Terry and I returned to Joy's to share the good news and invite her to let these ladies love her in Jesus's name. One person would organize everyone and oversee scheduling helpers for the family's daily needs: cooking, cleaning, transportation, homework, medical appointments, and help during sustained vomiting episodes.

Joy and Samuel talked and prayed and sensed that this miraculous, unexpected plan was from God. They committed to trust him with their family and this unborn child.

Timothy was born after nine months of combined, love-infused compassion and commitment.

Terry and I were privileged to be present at Timothy's birth. We prayed together as Joy held Timothy in her arms and expressed thanksgiving and praise to God for this precious child.

One year later, Joy invited everyone who helped them to Timothy's birthday party. She asked me to bring a video camera. She wanted to share their remarkable story with the women God used to save Timothy's life, and she wanted it recorded so that other ESL students and volunteer teachers could be blessed and encouraged by this neighborly example of love in action. That video has been shown hundreds of times throughout the United States in church-based ESL programs, touching many hearts, inspiring many to get involved in ESL, and to value life from the moment of conception forward.

Eighteen years later, Terry and I sat in a dimmed Goodwin Hall at Peabody Conservatory of Music in Baltimore to hear Timothy's senior cello recital. Timothy's concerts and awards are too long to list here. His cello expertise is exceptional. He has been accepted at Emory University in Atlanta to major in chemistry and minor in music. He wants to be a doctor.

Midway through an amazing hour of Stravinsky and Dvorak, I silently but joyfully cried as I remembered Joy's desperate phone call eighteen years ago and all that had happened since.

God, your outstretched arm rescued this little lamb. You placed Terry and me in the right place at the right time for the right reason to be your shepherding arms around this yet-to-be-born child and his family until the moment Timothy was born. What a gift and blessing he is and will become!

In my earthly ignorance, your plans were not what I wanted for myself. But I discovered that my grieving, my losses, and my shattered dreams are nothing compared to your perfect plan. I glimpsed how lovingly you were weaving your divine purposes for me and my children. I stumbled upon the truth that you are more than enough, more than everything I longed for that would never be enough.

You were weaving my life into the fabric of many other lives. Not for me to rescue them, but for them to humbly cry out to you: "I've had enough; Lord, help me discover that you are enough."

In ways we can only imagine, that ESL program has ministered to many thousands of internationals and hundreds of volunteers over the years. It has multiplied itself many times over in churches throughout the United States and in an ever-increasing number of countries around the world.

CHAPTER 35—ANDY'S CHOICES

In the summer of 1990, Andy and many church friends went to Saranac Lake, a Young Life camp in upstate New York. He was dating a vivacious blonde athlete named Susan from another high school who would also be at this camp with her friends. They continued dating into the fall of their sophomore year. One morning, I went to Andy's car to retrieve a package. An unanticipated spiritual prompting took my hand to the glove box where I found condoms. I pleaded, *Jesus, please show me what to do next.*

I approached his bedroom. I slowly turned the doorknob and was startled as he coldly stared back at me. I froze. *Oh, God. What happened?*

"Susan and I spent last night together, alone, at a hotel. I was planning to hurt myself when you left."

Struggling for words, I sat beside him. "Andy, thank you for telling me. I'm sorry you're hurting so badly. Hurting yourself is not the answer. You're my son. I love you unconditionally. Nothing you can do will cause me not to love you." As he rolled over to face the wall, I said, "I want you to come with me to see Dr. Morgan, the counselor. Talk to her. She can help."

Miraculously, I was able to reach Doris. "I can see Andy at noon. Bring him in." Together, Andy and I drove to the appointment.

Two hours later Doris said, "He's agreed to come back on Tuesday. Can you bring him?"

"Of course I will," I muttered as tears filled my eyes. She saw him until the crisis passed, but this was the first of many warnings of things to come.

He continued to date the same girl until her angry father called one evening. "Where are they? If she's not home by eleven, he's going to be in big trouble." That relationship ended.

After graduation, Andy had no plans.

In August 1992, Andy's best friend, Eric, and three other guys in their tight-knit group decided to go to Word of Life Bible Institute in Schroon Lake, New York. Roy, Eric's dad, persuaded Andy to join them for a year of Bible school beginning in September. Andy was eighteen. I managed to successfully apply for a Pell grant that enabled him to enroll.

Spiritual seeds planted in Andy's heart at Calvary Baptist blossomed in Word of Life's nurturing environment, and gradually drew him once again to the God who loved him unconditionally. Phone calls were full of excitement about what he was learning. Signs of depression disappeared, and happiness returned. He became good friends with Rachel, another Word of Lifer, a bubbly redhead from the Midwest, who loved the Lord and had a wonderful voice. He flew out to visit her the summer between school transitions. She seemed smitten with him, and he was fond of her, but his indecision ended the relationship.

Remarkably, that year's graduates all received full scholarships to Liberty University in Lynchburg, Virginia, from an anonymous donor. *"Praise God from whom all blessings flow."*[1]

Andy and his Word of Life friends carpooled to Liberty University on August 19, 1993, to start freshman semester. He was not academically prepared for college. He had partied, dated, and played sports through high school and ignored the academics. Too busy having a good time.

No surprise then, that structure, lectures, reading, and studying at the college level intimidated him. He skipped classes. Public speaking, a required course, triggered his panic attacks, and he refused to go to class. Shortly thereafter he withdrew from Liberty. I was stunned. Who walks away from a full scholarship to a four-year university? I tried to urge him to stick it out, but he'd made up his mind and came home in November.

He got odd jobs and floundered without purpose or direction. I suggested he take a sampling of aptitude tests to discover his innate giftings. He agreed. His scores were off-the-chart in differentiating musical tones and rhythms. Other measurements revealed a few elevated clusters in music-related business management and performance.

"This is great, Andy," I told him. "You can be a piano technician like your grandfather."

Well, that didn't sound cool. He dismissed the suggestion without discussion.

He continued with miscellaneous jobs and living at home off and on through the summer of 1996. He reconsidered working on pianos and talked to my Dad as dead ends appeared less and less attractive. This was well before cancer invaded Dad. He was still energetic and able to enjoy his grandson's company.

Dad introduced Andy to a nationally recognized piano technician school in Boston, where he could quickly learn what he needed to become a certified piano technician and start his own business. Dad offered to loan him the tuition fee and bought him a technician's case filled with tools he would need to get started. We funded room and board and miscellaneous expenses.

Andy and I drove to Boston that August to visit the school, find an apartment to rent, and get him enrolled in their one-year program beginning in September. We had fun touring the historic section of Boston where the North Bennett Street School was located and doing a little sightseeing. We drove home and returned to Boston with Mom, who wanted to give him a big send-off in her supercharged new car. Its big trunk was stuffed with bedding, clothing, and everything he would need for the apartment.

He had a great year. He loved everything about pianos and learning to make them sing at perfect pitch. His gifted ear could hear all the beats and temperaments required to bring the full keyboard of piano strings harmoniously up to perfect pitch. His manual dexterity, ability to shape and repair hundreds of small and large moving parts, and exacting skills with specialized woodworking and shaping tools were perfect for working on pianos. He had found his specialized occupation and became known as a gifted and talented piano technician.

Dad gathered the family together for a dinner at the retirement center's biggest dining room to celebrate Andy's graduation in late May 1997. He was giving Andy his business, which included piano tools and an extensive customer list built and maintained for thirty-two years. He wrote a retirement letter to all his customers and suggested they call Andy for their next scheduled tuning. He told them Andy was an excellent piano technician. Dad was so proud.

Dad was still unable to communicate love verbally or affectionately, but he continued to express it in ways he understood and could express. He consistently supported his daughters and grandchildren in gaining knowledge, skills, and opportunities that would help them succeed in life.

CHAPTER 36—A LIFE OF REGRETS

After Hank's passing in 1991, Mom became more mellow. She had a job supervising a security monitoring service out of her basement. The job could be tense at times, as security alarms would come in at all hours of the day and night. Her sleep was erratic until she convinced the owner to hire another person to help monitor incoming midnight-to-eight signals. She skillfully handled major alarms triggered during armed bank robberies, home invasions, and fires.

She stopped drinking for the sake of her job but continued to accumulate mountains of debt out of boredom and impulse shopping on QVC, a televised home shopping channel. I could never understand why banks kept her credit active. I guess it was because she always made the minimum payments, but the high interest rates meant the debt was always increasing instead of decreasing.

In 1992, she sold her house and moved into mine for a year until her new condo was ready. The condo was halfway between my home and Cassie's.

Her spending habits remained out of control until the day she could no longer make her minimum credit card payments and cover her other monthly expenses. The call finally came.

"Diana, you've got to come over here. I don't know what to do. You've got to help me figure out what to do."

I desperately didn't want to respond to her pleas. These things never ended well. She wanted to be rescued for the umpteenth time, and I was angry and frustrated with her irresponsible behavior.

After reviewing Mom's finances, declaring bankruptcy was the best option. My lawyer suggested we contact a reputable consumer protection agency to see if they would handle her case and negotiate a long-term manageable solution so she could remain in her condo. She had fifty thousand dollars in credit card debt in addition to her mortgage. It would be difficult, but if she cut up her cards and complied with the terms the consumer credit agency had negotiated with her creditors, she would be debt free in five years.

Miraculously, she worked hard and paid those debts, but she accumulated them again in the next five years. It was hopeless. I was finished with her finances, or so I thought.

It was 1999. I was fifty.

The final seven years of Mom's life were filled with constant physical pain. Arthritis in her knees, shoulders, and back had become debilitating, unbearable. She became a legal addict, dependent on opioid pain killers and frequent cortisone shots.

"Di, I only have eight pills left. That's only two days. Tomorrow is Friday. Do something! Call the doctor. Go over there. Find out where my pain pills are right now. I can't live without them. I'm in terrible pain. I wish the Lord would take me. I can't stand the pain." Her pain-fueled panic attacks became more frequent.

"My legs gave way when I got out of bed, and I can't get up. I've been sitting on the floor for hours. Come and help me get back in bed," she tearfully pleaded. It was 10:00 p.m. on a weeknight. I met Cassie and her husband, Jake, at Mom's in thirty minutes, and we managed to help her stand up and get back into bed.

She had wounds that wouldn't heal on her feet and legs. Occasionally her blood pressure would top two hundred forty over one hundred twenty, and I feared she would have a stroke. She was still supervising the security business by phone, trying to pay her bills.

Guilt and regret were her constant companions. Memories haunted her sleep. Still, she couldn't bring herself to acknowledge decades of dishonesty, abandonment, and selfishness or ask my forgiveness. She believed it was too late to change or make amends to her three daughters. She controlled her life in a powerful vise-grip, never letting go or relinquishing that control to God. Maybe she didn't trust Him, or maybe she didn't want to submit to anyone, not even God.

When she couldn't stand upright and walk anymore, her doctors sent her to a nearby hospital to find the cause. One afternoon, I was sitting behind her bed on a windowsill, beyond her view, reviewing what could happen next.

"Can't you come closer? Come sit next to me on the bed," she asked. I knew she was asking for a little affection since she was feeling alone and helpless, but I didn't respond. I couldn't. I still feel badly about that moment, even now as I write these words.

A week later, they transferred her to a rehab center to strengthen her leg muscles in hopes of sending her home. I followed behind the transport ambulance as it wound through the gently rolling farmland of northern Carroll County. I got Jessie on the phone and burst into uncontrollable weeping, worse than the day Dad married Lizzy. I could barely see the road through the tears. I wailed as loud as I could. Years of grief and pain roared out of me. I knew Mom would never return to her condo. This was the beginning of the end.

The next day, I looked for a nursing home that would admit her as a Medicaid patient. She dreaded going to a nursing home and rejected the few possibilities I found. She would be very miserable living in dormitory-like rooms of five or more Alzheimer patients waiting to die. She preferred to die rather than live like that.

"Mom, what do you want to take when I find a bed in a long-term-care facility?" I asked.

"My mink stole," she responded without hesitation.

"Why do you want your mink stole? What are you going to do with it?" I asked.

"I want to hang it on the wall at the foot of my bed and look at it. Remember all the good times." We laughed together wondering what the attendants would think.

"Hello. Is this Diana?" a nurse from the rehab center asked.

"Yes."

"We're transferring your mother back to the hospital. She has a high fever. Please come to the ER when you arrive."

It was midnight.

I called Terry and she drove with me to the ER. Mom was extremely sick. She had a urinary tract infection from being catheterized and was quickly succumbing to a systemic sepsis infection.

When Mom understood that without medication she would die quickly, she adamantly refused any treatment. The nurse called the doctor and asked us to leave the cubicle.

"Mary, do you know if you refuse treatment you will die? There is no need for you to die now. You'll recover within a few days," he explained.

"I don't want any medication. Nothing. I want to die. I know where I'm going, and I'm not afraid," she calmly responded.

It was a somber, short ride back to rehab in the morning to the room where she would soon pass from this life to the next. Terry and I were there. Cassie came and stayed. We waited. Mom slept off and on as she slipped into unconsciousness. When she looked uncomfortable, the nurse gave her morphine patches and unwound the compression bandages on her legs.

A hospice nurse came to speak to her one more time.

"Mary, it's not too late to reverse this. Do you want them to treat you with antibiotics, so you'll get better?" she asked.

"No. Don't you do anything," she said in her most determined voice. Those were the last words she uttered.

We got Jessie on the phone in Florida. Cassie had brought a hymnbook. The three of us sang her favorite hymns in harmony, like we did as children, for over an hour as her breathing became labored and shallow. I stood close to her ear, gave her a hug, and said, "I love you, Mom. You're doing a great job. It will all be over soon. No more pain."

Her body gradually relaxed. She took a few final breaths and peacefully slipped away into eternity on November 25, 2006. That's what she wanted. To be in control of her destiny until the very end.

Jessie came a week before Mom's memorial service at my church on December 2. One hundred and fifty people came—family, friends, and people she'd worked for and with over the years. Cousin Ed led the service. Cassie sang Mom's favorite hymns. I read her favorite Scripture passages.

Many young adult relatives and friends attending the service shared, "Your mother was so generous. She often gave us money on birthdays, holidays, or when we were needy. She'd always say, 'Don't tell Diana.'"

The whole room erupted in laughter, guests nodding knowingly at each other and looking in my direction. They had all experienced her generosity at least once over the years. No wonder she was in debt.

We three sisters spent the following week going through Mom's things. She would have enjoyed being with us as we took one entire day dividing her jewelry and bling. What a hoot! I had continuously scolded her for compulsively buying watches, rings, clothing, coats, purses, shoes, gadgets. Now I was taking those things home and happy to have them.

How ironic! An electric adjustable bed and cushy recliner, leather coats, sculptured lamps on pedestal tables, oriental rugs, leather sofas. On and on and on.

On our last day together in her condo, the UPS and FedEx delivery guys stopped by her building and knocked on her door, trying to deliver and pick up several boxes and packages.

"Your mother passed away? We're going to miss her. We come here almost every day to pick up or drop off packages. She was so nice."

The spare bedroom was full of unopened QVC boxes and others ready to return to sender.

We laughed until we cried. Yes, that was like Mom. Always wanting more stuff she didn't have yet. Or giving things away, which she couldn't afford because she was generous, and she wanted to. Giving was her love language. Spending beyond her means was one of her many weaknesses. Our mother was a charming enigma, and that's how she wanted to be remembered.

She wasn't certain about being cremated. But Aunt Marg, her sister, had been because it was less costly. OK, she would give her body to science, be cremated, and save us thousands of dollars.

When the Maryland Anatomy Board mailed her ashes to my post office box in Sykesville, I went to retrieve them. What a surreal experience. The cardboard box was heavier than I expected. She was now in my hands, my total control. What would I do with her? My sisters didn't want the ashes to be divided. Then I remembered how Mom bitterly complained for years that I didn't have any photo of her displayed in my home. I located a rustic wooden box Mr. Eareckson had given me many years ago. *Perfect*. I put Mom in it along with her death certificate and a few nostalgic photos of happy times and displayed the box in a prominent place in my living room right next to Dad's ceremonial burial flag.

Together again.

CHAPTER 37 — MICHAEL'S CHOICES

Sibling rivalry dominated Michael's relationship with Andy, who was four years older, taller, stronger, seemingly more skilled in team sports, and easily excelling in most things he attempted, except academics. Michael couldn't harness his jealousy and competitive spirit and occasionally struck out with fists, words, and projectiles.

Michael set out to make a name for himself. If the top was out of reach, he would race to the bottom and command attention from there. Public middle school was fertile soil for finding bottom dwellers, and Michael quickly took command of the troops. He discovered alcohol and became adept at getting and using it. By tenth grade (1994) he was an experienced substance abuser and petty peddler. Learning to drive expanded his territory, and his excesses with alcohol eventually dominated his life. He was out of control, ours and his. Nimble and cunning, he escaped many encounters with the police, and his behavior became risky.

In November, I called the police. "Our son is out of control, and we fear he is a danger to himself and others."

"We can't do anything until he commits an offense," the officer informed us.

"That's crazy. Prevention is better than jail or a funeral." No help from them.

On December 2, 1994, Michael got sick, and I took him to our family physician. "Do you want your mom to leave the room?" the doctor asked.

"No, she can stay," Michael answered.

The doctor listened as Michael voluntarily shared his story.

"I drive fast at night. Over 100 mph sometimes. I've thought about hitting a tree, no big deal."

More details spilled out. I don't remember them. I do remember wanting to vomit.

Thank you, Jesus. He's looked death in the eye and blinked. He's daring me to save him from himself. Lord, give me strength, I have none.

After the doctor visit, I convinced Michael to get evaluated for emotional/behavioral problems at a local inpatient medical facility with the help of the youth pastor at church. This seemed like our best option to possibly regain a smidgeon of control over his reckless behavior and pull Michael back from the brink of self-destruction. Several active issues were identified. The medical staff recommended that Michael enter an inpatient addiction rehab center for adolescents.

"No way!" he protested. "Nobody's gonna lock me up and tell me what to do!"

He rejected all offers of help to deal with his demons and regretted unmasking his inner fears. The momentary window of opportunity for receiving professional help closed as quickly as it opened.

Tom didn't want to do anything. "Wait and see," was his response. Wait to see my son's dead body wrapped around a tree? Or another parent's child bleeding under the wreckage of Michael's car? *Not on my watch.*

I decided to hide Michael's red Honda hatchback. Tom protested. I overruled him. I called Terry and together we hid the car where no one could find it. Cursing and rage spewed out when Michael discovered his car was gone.

After several days, the fury subsided. Until he needed a car to take out a girl from church. He borrowed Tom's car. After a youth meeting, driving down the winding driveway, looking at his date seated next to him, he hit a concrete lamppost base head on, totaling the car. An ambulance took the girl downtown to Shock Trauma, and Michael was taken to Howard County General Hospital with a severed bloody upper lip and broken front teeth. At the scene, I asked the police officer to give him a breathalyzer test, but his lip was too mangled. Michael lunged at me full of rage. Two EMTs restrained him and put him in the ambulance.

Terry and her husband drove me to the ER. I arrived to sounds of loud cursing directed at me from the triage room. The on-call maxillofacial surgeon numbed Michael's mouth, sewed his upper lip together, and repositioned and repaired four upper front teeth. Tom finally arrived but remained quiet and pensive.

Michael's facial swelling and bruising gradually decreased. The girl had a concussion, missed several weeks of school, but recovered. Tom's car was totaled.

The pastor offered to counsel Tom and me for several weeks to uncover the roots of obvious family dysfunction and to search for substance abuse programs to help Michael. He was still a minor at seventeen. We were legally responsible for him for twelve more months and could force him into a rehab program. Only one Christian rehab program in the country, Second Chance, in Memphis, Tennessee, accepted noncompliant minors, but there were several conditions. The total cost was sixteen thousand dollars paid in full upon arrival, and both parents must attend group therapy sessions two weekends a month until the adolescent was released from the program.

We contacted Second Chance, told them we would meet their requirements and bring Michael as soon as possible. They had a spot for him and agreed.

I organized an extended family meeting.

"Michael is out of control and abusing alcohol. He needs extended residential treatment for at least twelve months under twenty-four/seven surveillance and will be prevented from running away. The program's success rate is seventy-five percent. His life is on the line. We want to give him this chance. Will you help us pay for the program?"

Everyone gave money, even our friends. I raised the balance by selling treasured antiques given to me by others.

We planned a surprise departure the next morning and packed needed clothing, nothing else. Tom's brothers would go with us to keep Michael under control during the fourteen-hour trip.

Michael discovered the plan, packed his own duffel bag, and ran away before we woke up.

Fear gripped me. An unseen evil that wanted to kill my son descended upon me. Overpowered by grief, my mind and speech were muted. Only guttural moans came out as I rocked back and forth in a fetal position on the carpet next to his disheveled bed. This continued for hours until Terry covered me with a blanket and put a tape recorder next to my head, softly playing "I Will Be with You," a favorite song. I drifted off to sleep.

CHAPTER 38—FLIGHT TO RECOVERY

With Michael missing, my supercharged rescue mode kicked in full force. "Terry, please call our closest family and friends and ask them to pray."

"Will do."

"Call everyone Michael knows, especially the likely co-conspirators," I snapped at Tom. "Mom knows a private investigator—call her and get him on the phone."

After several hours, we concluded that if anyone knew where Michael was, they weren't saying.

Another dilemma loomed large. How would we get Michael to Memphis once we found him? He'd be furious. Too strong for us to handle. We'd never get him in the car, let alone keep him in the car for the drive to Memphis.

I called every commercial airline flying from Baltimore to Memphis. "We need to transport a noncompliant adolescent to Memphis. Can you accommodate him on your airline?"

"Only if you can guarantee he will not resist or disrupt the flight." FAA regulations. Blah, blah, blah.

That was not an option. Standing at the top of the hill behind our home, I lifted my voice and my hands to the sky. "Lord. Please. Help."

I heard, then saw across the pasture and above the tree line, a twin-engine plane flying toward me. *That's it! We could hire a private plane to fly Michael to Memphis. Thank you, Jesus.*

"Tom, call, John. See if he's willing to fly to Memphis with us and, if necessary, keep Michael in a hammerlock all the way." John was Tom's employee and a former Maryland State wrestling contender.

He agreed to come.

I called Martin State Airport, a small public-use airport. "Yes, we can have a twin-engine plane and a pilot on call when you have Michael in custody. He'll meet your group in Frederick. Please bring a person who can physically control him if he gets agitated."

Now, how to get Michael to the municipal airport in Frederick? "Terry, please call several elders from church and ask them to be on call to caravan with us from Sykesville to Frederick in case Michael tries to jump out of our car."

"You've got it," she promised.

I called Dad. He agreed to pay for the flight, wanting to help save Michael from self-destruction. Tom, the wrestling champ, and I would fly with Michael to Memphis, leave him at Second Chance and fly back to Baltimore.

We had a plan.

Meanwhile, the private investigator scoured Michael's familiar hangouts. Nothing. He clandestinely monitored phone calls, followed the most likely suspects, checked criminal records, parked his car near suspicious locations, watched and waited.

On the seventh day the runaway called Tom. "I'm OK, Dad." He sounded like he wanted to be rescued again. The police traced the call and tracked him to a friend's grandmother's house. She had been out of town for the week, was now home, and wanted this groggy teenager off her living room sofa.

A policeman put him in a cruiser and drove him home. The men from church arrived after dark. The policeman put Michael and his duffel bag in our car. With the wrestling champ seated next to him, the caravan left for the rendezvous point twenty miles west in Frederick.

A Hollywood movie thriller in reality. Pitch black midnight, other than two strands of bright runway lights and a small glimmer from the control tower. Three caravan vehicles, engines idling, dimmers on, their exhaust crystalizing in the chilly air. People bundled up, waiting, sipping coffee, praying, others chatting in hushed tones.

The plane circled the runway and landed. The stairway dropped. The pilot greeted us, took on more fuel, shook our hands, and said, "Let's go."

Michael asked to sit next to the pilot. The champ buckled him into the copilot seat and sat right behind him. Tom and I buckled up in the back. As the plane revved its engines, rolled down the runway, and lifted us above the cloud cover into the moonlit night, God seemed closer than ever before. The reassuring words of "I Will Be with You" once again calmed my fears and lulled me into a peaceful sleep.

"Hey, Mom. Wake up. Look," Michael whispered, pointing out the window with a gentle, childlike grin.

Dawn lit the horizon. We were cocooned by cumulonimbus clouds on all sides that dwarfed the plane and draped the sky in gold, orange, rose, and beige hues, like a heavenly cathedral. I've never seen anything so majestic before or since. God with us. The dawning of a young life rescued from death's determined grip by the power of the living God who hears and answers prayer and freely pours out his grace on the most undeserving.

"Praise God from whom all blessings flow."[1] "And call on me in the day of trouble; I will deliver you, and you will honor me" (Ps. 50:15).

CHAPTER 39—SECOND CHANCE

Second Chance occupied a large, converted warehouse on the edge of Memphis. Two floors, no windows, few doors, but cheerfully signed with its logo and positive slogans. A long carpool was queued at the entrance. Adolescents were exiting each car, three by three, one holding onto the belt of the newbie as the trios entered the building.

Our foursome found the admission officer. We filled out and signed papers, handed him a check, received a large packet of information, met the executive director and his wife, said our goodbyes, and left Michael in their custody.

We taxied back to the airport, boarded the plane, and I slept until we were back in Frederick.

Michael remained in the program twelve months. He lived in private homes with local families who had adolescents also enrolled in the program. Every family involved at Second Chance, local or out of state, tenaciously clung to the lifeline the program represented and followed its principles. Daily group sessions, individual psychotherapy, church twice on Sundays. Public school attendance if the kid was compliant, home school, if not. Bimonthly weekend visits from parents providing the structure necessary for recovery.

Tom and I traveled to Memphis twice a month by plane or car, stayed with relatives to save money, participated in meaningful group therapy sessions with other parents on Saturdays, and saw Michael from a distance during the church service on Sundays. Eventually, he overnighted offsite with us on weekend visits. Even when he turned eighteen and was free to leave, he chose to remain until his recovery plan was completed, and he graduated from the local high school in May 1996.

Immediately after the graduation ceremony, Michael embraced both of us and said, "Mom and Dad, thanks for bringing me to Second Chance. For giving me a chance to learn from my mistakes, make better choices, and finish high school. I'm grateful to be alive. I love you."

Michael enrolled in a welding course in Cincinnati, Ohio, and got certified. He worked at different jobs until he launched his own landscaping business.

We were left with significant credit card debt for travel expenses—plane tickets, gas, food, and hotels. But worth the money. How could we put a price on his life? We would have done anything to give him this chance at recovery. God had moved immovable mountains and brought Michael back from the jaws of destruction. We were forever grateful to our family, friends, Second Chance, and the God who hears and answers prayer. Brokenness had become a strange unwelcome friend, pointing me toward the God I love and refining and molding me into who I was becoming.

> Consider it pure joy, my brothers and sisters,
> whenever you face trials of many kinds,
> because you know that the testing of your faith
> produces perseverance.
> Let perseverance finish its work
> so that you may be mature and complete,
> not lacking anything. (James 1:2–4)

CHAPTER 40—ETHIOPIA AND BEYOND

In Joni's absence, a latent desire to engage disability persisted, but a new context was needed. My two sons were teenagers, my marriage had atrophied, and a bold new adventure might be what I needed to rejuvenate my longing for purpose and meaning. Terry and her husband had been Peace Corp workers in Ethiopia in the sixties. For ten years, she had persistently pushed the possibility of a return visit to Ethiopia to explore ministry opportunities. I agreed to go to shut her up.

One step out of the walled mission compound in Addis Ababa plunged me into a world of stench and desperation. My eyes darted away from grotesque human forms as I was engulfed by extended arms and grasping hands. Assaulted. Repulsed. Nauseated. My comfort zone violated. I fled back inside the safety of concrete walls topped with barbed wire and glass to catch my breath. *What happened?*

Culture shock. Shock that exposed the pretense I could do anything to relieve such misery. I was ignorant, inadequate. Unprepared to comprehend the magnitude and complexity of the problem, let alone do anything to make a difference. I hid in my room for days, immobilized.

Facing this ugly reality about myself was the first step in entering the helpless world of suffering humanity.

∅

I was initially overwhelmed by culture shock being in Ethiopia. Taking care of Joni for twelve years was light years removed from leprosy-ridden body parts of homeless outcasts who lay on the street corners, and puss-filled, fly-infested eyes of half-naked children grabbing my arms, begging, "Mother. Mother. Bread. Hungry."

I gradually began to see that I had stepped through an enormous door of opportunity. An opportunity for me to share and give back what had been given to me in a new context on a new continent with thousands of people I was yet to meet.

Terry and I decided to cofound a nonprofit organization, The Global Transformation Network, Inc. after weeks of prayer and discussion focused on disability issues in Africa, beginning in Ethiopia. After six months of research, planning, and paperwork, we were official, and the real work commenced. We developed materials, opened an office in Addis Ababa, hired and trained staff, cast the vision of advocacy for persons with disabilities, and conducted seminars, workshops, and trainings.

We have given disability trainings in and out of Ethiopia many times since 2000, adding other countries in East and West Africa, holding a strategic meeting with multi-national South American trainers in Argentina, and taking a two-week trip to China to visit a Christian adoption agency in Hong Kong and an orphanage/training center for abandoned deaf children further inland. We networked with other mission agencies, international organizations, and associations. For twelve years, we enjoyed our collaboration with Perspectives on the World Christian Movement as instructors of community development in their sixteen-week course on world missions. We taught this topic for classes in the mid-Atlantic region.

We enjoy every opportunity to train and equip others in the pursuit of their spiritual calling.

CHAPTER 41—THE DREAM ADDITION

In 2000, our thirty-year home mortgage was *paid in full*. In retrospect, we should have had a big party and celebrated that achievement. The house we had lovingly built together and dedicated to serving others was now ours.

But things had changed. Dad had passed away. Lizzy was still alive. Mom was stable. Andy was newly married to Anna, both with promising occupations and incomes. Michael was three years beyond his recovery, living with us, working full-time, and planning to start his own lawn care business. And Terry and I had recently founded a nonprofit organization focused on advocacy for persons with disabilities in Africa.

Tom had not changed. He was still an Eeyore—pessimistic, gloomy, depressed, and stuck in underpaid jobs.

Andy and Anna had purchased a beautiful home plus two rental properties. Her sales job, his piano tuning business, and their joint real-estate investments and rentals were all lucrative. But success required space, and Andy needed workshop space for his piano restoration and repair operation.

Michael wanted to buy equipment and supplies to start his landscaping business and needed a big garage and storage space for vehicles, mowers, and more. The new nonprofit needed office space, and Tom needed space for his woodworking tools and materials. All these enterprises required a lot of square footage. We got a big idea. Tom and I designed a two-story, four-thousand-square-foot addition that included an oversized two-vehicle garage with automated doors. There would be enough space for everyone's enterprises, and we would each share our proportional part of the refinanced mortgage. We could build the addition ourselves, at cost, saving thousands of dollars. Tom drew the detailed architectural plans and both of us physically worked on a long list of external and internal subcontractor-type jobs.

As site manager, I would handle the daily coming and going of subcontractors, run errands, facilitate permits and inspections from the county, pick up materials at the local lumber yard, and troubleshoot as needed. As in the past, Tom and I worked well together on this type of project. And we were spurred on by our belief that this would increase the value of our home, and therefore, our retirement fund when the house was sold in the distant future.

It was impressive—optimally functional and adequate for everyone's needs. Paying the collective mortgage was stress-free for everyone. Until things changed. Again.

CHAPTER 42—THE ADDITION NIGHTMARE

Mom had accumulated another mountain of debt before her passing in 2006. She could no longer work long hours after hitting seventy and developing multiple health problems.

I'd approached Jessie then about buying Mom's condo. "It's a good investment, relatively new, and a great location. If she sold it to one of us, she could pay off her mortgage and debts and transfer the remaining cash to the three of us for safe keeping. She would continue making mortgage payments with her salary. The property would appreciate and generate passive income for you. Think about it."

"Sorry, Di, we're investing in commercial property for Joe's medical practice and helping the kids with their tuitions."

Next, I approached Cassie. "Sounds like a great idea, but Jake says no. Sorry."

Unwisely, Tom and I bought Mom's condo with another mortgage on our home. She had continued to live there, sending us the rent until her death. Our monthly mortgage payment had doubled.

While we were discussing Mom's condo, things were

unraveling for Andy and Anna. There had been hints of estrangement, but one day she said to him, "I don't know what I was thinking, marrying a piano tuner." Andy's self-esteem crashed. He begged her to join him in marriage therapy. She went through the motions for several sessions but clearly didn't want to restore the relationship. It seemed like she was looking for the right moment to announce she was leaving.

Once the addition was finished in 2000, Michael had claimed the fifteen-hundred-square-foot loft for his own living space and committed to pay his portion of the mortgage. He also claimed half of the garage and the barn for his equipment and was set to build his future.

Michael married Janice in 2005. She loves to cook, knit, do crafts, and throw elaborate parties for our family gatherings. In 2009, the twins, Micah and Maya, were born. What love and joy they brought into our home! A swimming pool, a vegetable garden, craft projects, battery-powered jeeps, swings with climbers and sandboxes, a large chicken coop with a rooster and several hens, three cats and a dog, and many other delightful childhood activities filled our lives once again.

We celebrated holidays and birthdays with fun and fanfare, but especially Christmas. On Christmas morning, parents and grandparents gathered around the tree to witness excited giggles and raucous laughter as the twins tore open wrapped gifts and threw paper in every direction. Family stayed all day, talking, helping with the turkey and fixings, snitching a taste of gourmet desserts before the scrumptious feast, helping with the cleanup, and cheering for favorite football teams.

One Christmas was particularly memorable. We all agreed

Tom and I would get up early and join Michael, Janice, and the twins to open gifts under their tree. On Christmas Eve, I had wrapped our gifts but left them hidden until morning. At six o'clock, we would carry them upstairs and put them under their tree.

At five o'clock Christmas morning, I heard the kitchen door open. Little footsteps headed for the living room. Then they came racing down the hallway to my bedroom.

"Granny, there's nothin' under the Christmas tree! Nothin'!" Micah yelled throwing his arms up and out and down to the floor. "Nothin'! Nothin'!"

"Oh, Micah. Don't worry. Santa had a lot of houses to visit last night. We must be last on his list. It's still early. Don't worry; he'll find us."

D

After Anna packed her suitcases in 2003 and announced she was filing for divorce, Andy drank excessively. I couldn't seem to reach him as he descended into a dark place. He gave in to Anna's demands in the divorce settlement. They put the big house up for sale, while Andy temporarily stayed there, uncertain what to do, numb with pain and alcohol.

A woman named Tracy appeared unannounced one day to get a sales tour of their house. No realtor present. Her story was full of inconsistencies, but Andy was in no shape to recognize it. When Tracy flirted with him, he was defenseless and vulnerable.

My bookkeeper had told me his ex-wife was crazy—a danger to herself and everyone who came near her. By the time I got home, I concluded this mysterious Tracy was the ex-wife. My legs buckled as I sank to the bedroom floor, numb with fear. I desperately cried out, *Help, Lord. Deliver us from this evil. Spare the life of my son, Andy, as you spared Michael's. Give me strength.*

Weeks later, my handsome, winsome, talented son

stopped by our home to get a few things. He was moving in with Tracy. "Whatever you do," I told him, "don't let her into your heart." The look on his face, a peculiar grin I had never seen before, frightened me. I sensed her demons were already oppressing his mind and heart. I couldn't imagine what horror and heartache would engulf all of us that day, but I sensed it had already arrived.

I pulled all the fire alarms and donned my first-responder hardhat. I was going to put up the fight of my life for Andy. Remnants of *I can do this, I can rescue him from this raging inferno* still deceived me. I persuaded Andy to sign an exhaustive power of attorney and medical directive appointing me as his agent for both. He had to sign the divorce papers, but I acted as his power of attorney for everything else. Andy and Anna's rental homes were sold. He was now flush with cash, which he foolishly lavished on Tracy until it was gone several years later. Consequently, he stopped paying his share of the mortgage on the addition built for his piano shop, plunging Tom and me into panic mode.

The chaos of their relationship spilled over onto Tom, Michael, and me in every imaginable way. Andy stood by passively as Tracy bruised and bloodied him many times. He never protected himself or raised an arm in defense. We later discovered she was manic-depressive, would not take her meds, and had been a substance abuser for years. Her arrest sheet and run-ins with the law were extensive. There were frequent warrants out for her arrest.

One dreadful day, Andy stopped by his piano shop at our house. Unexpectedly, Tracy drove up the driveway in a new SUV Andy had purchased for her use. Alarmed, I marched over to the vehicle and viciously pounded on the driver's window with clenched fists until both hands were black and blue.

"If you don't leave my son alone, I'm going to kill you," I screamed over and over. I have never been so out of control with such unbridled hatred and rage before or since.

Andy suddenly appeared and moved me away from the car. Tracy backed up, turned around, and sped away. Fifteen minutes later, again with a packed duffel bag, he got into his car to follow her. I almost died that day from uncontrollable rage and a broken heart. I am still living with the physical ramifications of all the trauma.

While Terry and I were in Ethiopia for a month in 2004, I got a call from Andy. He had found a suspicious lump that needed to be surgically removed. The probability of the lump being cancerous was 99 percent. I anxiously awaited the pathology report. Several days later, the result was definitive. Benign. I cried for a long time.

Unknown to me, Tracy was his caregiver. When pain pills ran out, and the pain persisted, she arranged for more opioids. Then more. Andy quickly became addicted. We were now statistics, unwilling members of the alien world of substance abuse many others have experienced. Ignorant. Helpless. Frightened. Staring into an unknown abyss. Struggling to hold on to hope.

As I write, Andy is in recovery and doing well. He's rebuilding the life and business he lost and conquering each demon one by one. He may write his own book. We may even write a book together from the mother/son perspective. For now, I've said enough. I've finally learned how to let go and let God. I now know this is not a cliché—it is a roadmap for the rest of my life.

Tracy died in February 2019.

Amid these events, on January 6, 2004, Tom's father

passed away in Newark, New Jersey, after a prolonged illness. Before his death, I visited him at the hospital to make one more effort to persuade him to speak to each of his five children and settle any unresolved issues among them from the past. He wouldn't make eye contact or respond to my suggestion just like he had done the day Tom and I announced our engagement in his living room.

That was the last time I spoke to him.

From my perspective, Tom's parents' dedication to sixty-plus years of church ministry always took priority over the needs of their children. I believe their motives and intentions were not purposefully harmful, but many unintended consequences grew out of their undying obedience and loyalty to their spiritual callings as pastor and pastor's wife. In my opinion, this left lifelong emotional scars in Tom.

Tony, Tom's youngest brother who is now deceased, told me that on the day his father died, he sat by his dad's lifeless body in the hospital room behind a closed door until the undertaker came. He spent several hours screaming at his father, disgorging the pent-up anger, frustration, and pain that he could not share while his father was alive.

Recently, Martha passed away at ninety-six after many serious illnesses and other heartbreaks over the struggles of her children and grandchildren. She had learned to be resilient and kept living until old age finally exhausted her body, and Jesus took her home.

CHAPTER 43–UPROOTED

Tom and I planted our first blue spruce Christmas tree in the front yard in 1971, even before we finished building our house. By 2014, the evergreen was fifty feet tall. The years had not been kind to it. Snowstorms and ice, too heavy for its limbs to bear, tore away big sections, and caterpillar infestations destroyed branches from top to bottom. But it had been a sturdy sheltering home for many critters—furry, feathered, and creepy. It continued to put out new mint green bristles and grew very robust. It was no longer beautiful, but it had survived.

Likewise, our home had become a shelter for family, friends, and the temporarily homeless on many occasions. We were grateful and hopeful in the beginning, full of good will and generosity, plans and prayers. The dream was beautiful. But as the pace of change accelerated, requests for help became audible cries for more extensive assistance.

"I lost my job. Can I stay with you for a while?"

"Our landlord evicted our family from our rental house. Can you put us up for a few weeks until we find another place?"

"Phil can't stay with his folks anymore. Can he stay here for a while?"

At times the house become so full that I put out a No Vacancy sign. Space and privacy were hard to find, the parking area needed enlarging, the septic tank needed more frequent emptying, and the electric bill reflected the ever-increasing number of showers, tubs of laundry, and heavy-duty heating and air conditioning use. These added expenses depleted our meager savings and moved us ever closer to bankruptcy.

After his divorce, Andy's portion of the mortgage payment dwindled and stopped.

Michael's business was struggling in spite of years of hard work, seeking counsel, expanding and shrinking his lawn care services. His contributions to the mortgage payment also decreased with the economic tidal waves and the birth of the twins in 1999.

Tom's depression, job changes, and accumulating aches and pains—combined with the fluctuations in the housing and remodeling markets—sent his income on a downhill trajectory.

The nonprofit organization Terry and I had started provided a consistent modest income for me plus health insurance. But this required sustained effort to raise funding for our ministries in Africa. Fundraising is not one of my strengths.

When Mom passed away, we rented her condo to cover the mortgage and property taxes. This worked well until our wonderful renters moved out, and the real estate market tanked. Rents decreased, and we started to lose money. We put the condo up for sale. It finally sold in July 2009. We tried to make a large prepayment to renegotiate our River Road mortgage with those funds, but the lender hung up on us. The subprime mortgage crisis of 2007 and 2008 and subsequent recession forced us into survival mode. We kept the cash and used it for seven years to maintain the status quo.

We were on a slow walk to bankruptcy. *Have mercy, Lord. How can I endure more pain, more losses, more grieving? I've had enough already!*

I had become a modern-day Job, pleading for help, wanting answers, and getting God questions in response.

Having lost everything, Job had uttered, "Though he slay me, yet will I hope in him" (Job 13:15).

Lord, if I adopt Job's attitude, will my sustained suffering cease? I knew Job's response was correct, but I couldn't figure out how he untangled the seeming inconsistencies. Paul tackled it this way: "We are hard pressed on every side, but not crushed; perplexed, but not in despair; persecuted, but not abandoned; struck down, but not destroyed" (2 Cor. 4:8–9).

I had more to learn, but I was dreading it.

In February 2015, Tom finally agreed we had no choice but to leave our beautiful homestead. We had many regrets, fears, and what-ifs, but tried to console ourselves with lots of we-did-all-we-coulds. We put the house up for sale. It sat on the market for a year because we listed it for a higher price than was recommended. At the same time, we were looking for temporary housing. Our choices were limited.

Emptying the house was a nightmare. Forty-five years of the occasionally-valuable-but-mostly-worthless hodgepodge was daunting. Ten people. Four businesses. An assortment of pets and chickens. Landscaping and snow removal equipment. Lots of grand and upright pianos, repair tools, and supplies. Wood and woodworking tools and machinery. Picture-framing benches, tools, and materials. A canoe, swing set, sandbox, sliding board, and swimming pool. New homes needed to be found for everyone and everything except for what was sold and the van loads of junk that went to the county dump.

Michael and his family had already relocated. They bought a townhouse in western Maryland and moved the landscaping business to an industrial site along Interstate 70.

Andy needed to move all his piano tools and piano inventory to another location and find a place to live.

Tom's depression became disabling. He was confused, oppositional, and seemingly unable to decide what to do with his sixty-year hoard of accumulated stuff—including file cabinets and boxes of papers from two previous business enterprises.

I methodically proceeded to do the next thing with my belongings and stacks of paper until I finished each task.

At the same time, we were working through a separation agreement, inching toward a final divorce decree. Given the circumstances between us, it seemed ill-advised to continue cohabiting in another home after this one sold.

One dense foggy night was poignantly memorable. Anxious and depressed, I retreated to an upper porch and sat alone in sullen silence. This scene is usually wonderful at night—big bright moon, silhouettes of horses munching grass, and fireflies speckled across the fields as crickets hum in unified crescendos signaling all is well. But that night, all I could identify was a faint spotlight in the distance overhanging the end of a neighbor's barn with a diminishing hazy halo. I could barely make out a narrow, dimly lit path across the pasture between that light and where I was sitting.

Please speak to me, Lord. I know you're here.

He focused my conscious musings on this assurance: "Your word is a lamp for my feet, a light on my path" (Ps. 119:105).

I recalled and then recited in worshipful tones the Bible promises I had memorized years ago. Gradually, his peace soothed my soul as I remembered how loved and secure I am in Christ. The emotional fog lifted as tense muscles loosened and troubling doubts drifted away.

That night, I knew I was not alone and found comfort in God's presence. I was finding my way by following the path he was illuminating in front of me.

We finally had a buyer and a settlement date, April 22, 2016. The sale price was significantly less than we had hoped for, but we had no choice. We faced bankruptcy if we did not accept the offer.

Moving day arrived quickly. The long-dreaded moment had come for me to leave our cherished homestead. I had no more tears, but a heavy sadness pressed on my lungs. I labored to catch my breath as I slowly drifted down the winding driveway lined with locust and sycamore trees and yellow daffodils for the last time. I'm still sorrowful when I remember that place. Grieving takes time. Take it.

My persistent can-do defiance had been reduced to ashes with the sale of our home. Its inescapable loss incinerated the lie that I could control any adversity that came my way. *Truth to self—I am utterly helpless.*

Questions about Job returned. What did Job mean when he had this insight at the end of his ancient story of suffering? "My ears had heard of you, but now my eyes have seen you" (Job 42:5)?

Could it be that my lifelong crucible of suffering was God's uniquely designed rite of passage leading me to the coveted prize? I had heard (and known) about God all my life. Now I was seeing and experiencing him more up close and personal with each pain and loss I endured as he lovingly carried me through every heartache.

CHAPTER 44-DIVORCE

God said he hated divorce in Malachi 2:16; therefore, I hated divorce.

I meant it when I made this solemn vow before God, family, and friends on June 26, 1971, "For better or worse, richer or poorer, in sickness and health until death do us part."

I especially hated divorce because of my mother's adultery, my father's choice when he married Lizzy, and all the unintended, inevitable, negative consequences visited upon my sisters, my children, and myself that linger still.

I vowed to myself, *Not me. I won't let this happen to me. I will hang in until the bitter end before I will admit failure and violate my marriage vows.*

But the drip, drip, drip, of Tom's rejection over forty-five years of marriage wore away my inner core despite all my attempts to allow Christ to be my wellspring of love and sustenance.

We had tried marital therapy from 1980 to1982, and again from 2015 to 2016, but nothing changed in our relationship. I sought the help of a succession of behavioral therapists over the years, seeking sanity, clarity, and healthy ways to endure the unendurable.

In 2012, I discovered Regeneration, a nonprofit organization in Baltimore that offered a self-help group called Just for Wives. This group met every two weeks on Monday nights for many years and provided a haven for hurting women trapped in complex marital situations. They offered many helpful resources, therapists, support groups, targeted programs for various issues, and many books and articles.

For the first time, at Just for Wives, I found a safe place among women with shared heartaches and pent-up pain and confusion. We could express our common experiences openly and honestly. It was a very healing time.

I decided to explore biblically sanctioned reasons for divorce as I saw the best years of my life being consumed by cycles of feeling unloved, unfulfilled, unappreciated, unaffirmed, rejected, blamed, shamed, mocked, and ignored. If I had biblical grounds for divorce, I would seek God's direction for the final chapters of a life yet to be lived. I was sixty-seven.

"Di, you've had biblical cause for divorce for the last twenty-five years," Bonnie said.

"What do you mean, Bon?" I responded.

"Tom emotionally abandoned you years ago, and in 1990, he physically abandoned you, right?"

"Yes."

"Well, it's now 2015. Don't you suppose it's time to at least consider getting a divorce?" she continued.

"I've considered it many times. I promised myself I would never do what my mother did. I would never precipitate a divorce. God hates divorce," I emphatically stated.

"God hates infidelity and abandonment too. He permits divorce for those two reasons. Aren't four decades of living with Tom—the rejection, the physical and emotional abandonment, and the pain—enough?" she reasoned.

I consulted three respected pastors and one elder/trainer who had all known Tom and me for many decades. I searched the Presbyterian Church of America's General Assembly Paper Archives and found one research study entitled *Report of the Ad-Interim Committee on Divorce and Remarriage to the 20th General Assembly*.[1] I read and studied the entire

293-page paper, reviewing every Bible passage mentioned. I needed confidence I was not violating a fundamental biblical principle in the process if I was going to seriously consider the possibility of divorce.

After exhaustive research and many lengthy conversations with three pastors and an elder, including their wives, I was at peace about the possibility of divorce.

"Tom, it's time for us to try marital therapy again to see if we can find a way to continue on together," I pressed.

He agreed after putting up mild resistance. He too was tired of the status quo and was finally ready to sort things out between us. We saw Joe, a therapist I had seen off and on for years, who knew much of our story already. Tom liked Joe and was comfortable being vulnerable with him both in our joint sessions and in sessions alone with Joe.

"When I said I didn't want to have sex with you anymore in 1990, I didn't mean never. Why didn't you ever bring it up again?" he queried, with a tone of obvious accusation.

I leaned forward in my chair, looked him in the eyes and raised my voice in disbelief.

"You expected *me* to bring that up again? Do you have any idea how devastating that declaration was after enduring decades of your rejection and ridicule? You were expecting *me* to bring it up again? Why didn't *you* bring it up?"

I was so angry I could barely contain myself.

"Tom, it is *twenty-six years* later. Is this all you have to say to me? Why couldn't *I* read *your* mind? Why didn't *I* fix *your* declaration of physical desertion of *me*? Unbelievable!"

I finally had the courage to exhale the outrage and humiliation I had silently held in for twenty-six estranged years. We drove home in separate cars. I cried and groaned out loud the whole way.

God promised that my deepest longings would be satisfied, wounds mended, ashes turned into something beautiful. How was that working for me? Would I receive those promises in this world or only in the next?

CHAPTER 45—A LETTER TO MY FAITHFUL FAMILY AND FRIENDS

On March 22, 2016, our forty-five years of marriage came to an end. It has been a long and rocky road for both of us, and necessary endings are sometimes a harsh reality that must be accepted. Even after several serious attempts at counseling over the years and pausing for reconsideration at the divorce settlement signing table, Tom once again stated that he believed it was too late. Tom has expressed his regret over this outcome. I am yielding to the Spirit's promptings to identify my own false idols of needing to be right and needing to see myself as *without fault* in this whole thing. The Spirit took the truth of Jonah 2:8 and drove it right into my heart and conscience: "Those who cling to worthless idols turn away from God's love for them." I was compelled, after much internal struggle, to ask Tom for forgiveness for my part in this and to give forgiveness in return. I do not want to forfeit the grace that could be mine by clinging to worthless pride and arrogant self-righteousness.

In this very spot, God has gloriously triumphed over my sinful nature and given me an extra measure of grace to do what seemed impossible. Almost immediately after I surrendered to the Spirit on the forgiveness issue, several things that have tormented me for so long began to move toward resolutions.

Settlement with the new buyers of our home happened on April 22. The culmination of all our wise and not-so-wise decisions brought us to this place, and we must accept its meager reality, let go of the regrets, and move forward. Please pray we can be gracious with each other as we struggle through this final heavy dose of reality and its consequences.

As you can imagine, there are many details to work out, wrap up, and reorganize as we go from being married to single again. Please leave the communication to us—we prefer to speak directly with people and not leave our situation to random gossip, which tends to be inaccurate.

Tom and I remain amicable and are working together to close this chapter of our lives and to begin new ones. There is no shock value in our story—there are no salacious facts to uncover. I hope no one goes looking for secrets or foolishly indulges their imaginations. Ours is a long, sad, painful story of thousands of missed opportunities to pursue personal inner transformation in order to experience a healthy marital relationship, to loosen our grip on worthless idols, and to open ourselves up to receive the grace that could have been ours and that could have healed us and our marriage. As you can imagine, we are both physically and emotionally exhausted by the magnitude of all these changes and transitions happening simultaneously.

For those of you who may be in marital turmoil right now, I urge you to take the long view of your relationship as you consider what has happened to us. A whole lifetime of enjoying God's graces available in the marital relationship has passed us by, never to be relived. Our marriage didn't need to end this way but it has. I pray the end of your journey will be different.

I love and appreciate you very much. I am grateful for your prayers, support, and friendship through the ups and downs of life. The book *Pilgrim's Progress* comes to mind: how Pilgrim, on his perilous journey to the Beautiful Place, encountered many menacing, frightening, deceiving, challenging, and dangerous characters and frequent hazardous bends in the road—until he finally made it to his ultimate destination, heaven. God has graced me with family and special friends like you to share that journey with me on the way to our final destination. I am truly blessed.

With much love and affection,
Diana

CHAPTER 46—SEASON OF BIG TRANSITIONS

I had made preliminary plans to store my things and live at Cousin Rachel and Ed's home in Pennsylvania after selling our house—until the location of my new home became clear. However, I had more options regarding my next home as the total amount of my inheritance from Dad became clearer.

Unexpectedly, I learned I might have enough assets to move into the retirement community where Dad had been living when he passed away. Miracles were few and far between in my life, but I experienced one as I met with the finance people. "Yes, your financial assets qualify you for acceptance into our retirement community," they told me.

I then chatted with the sales folks. "Yes, we have a studio apartment ready for you to move into."

"I'll take it," I replied.

Our divorce was final on April 16. I moved into a refurbished studio apartment on the large retirement campus on April 21 and finalized the sale of River Road the next day. God's perfect timing. Tom put his stuff into storage and spent the next year at his sister's home in South Carolina to help care for his aging mother.

$\mathcal{D}$

"Welcome to your new home," was a constant greeting from hundreds of my new neighbors. Every time I came through the main gate and entered this wonderful community, I pinched myself (I still do!), hardly able to believe that God made a way for me to be here. More than twenty-one hundred retired residents live on this beautiful campus, and more than one thousand employees serve them daily.

I quickly unpacked, set up a home office, and trusted that God would carry me gently through all this latest round of transitions I faced. Large house to tiny studio apartment. Handful of neighbors to more than two thousand neighbors. A horse pasture on a gently rolling hill in western Howard County to a sprawling retirement campus on the western edge of Baltimore City. Living with ten people, three cats, and a dog, to living alone.

In the fall of 2016, I discovered a persistent infection in two sweat glands on my right thigh. Frequent rounds of antibiotics and outpatient lancing had not resolved the recurring infection.

Note to self: Don't ignore the little things. God uses them as warning signs of something more challenging around the next bend in the road.

On October 24, I saw the surgeon again. "The tissue was benign, but they might need to be surgically removed if the infection persists. When was the last time you had a mammogram?"

"I don't remember," I admitted. "Years ago."

He sent me next door to radiology where they performed the procedure immediately. The radiologist saw something, but it was small and unremarkable; she suggested I come back in six months.

But when I told Terry, she insisted that I go to Mercy Hospital where she continues to be monitored for a possible breast cancer recurrence after her personal experience more than thirty years ago.

I made an appointment, but soon my body struck back in a new way. It had reached its breaking point. Physical complaints became too intense and sustained to be ignored. The consequences of decades of high-decibel, nonstop stress and emotional chaos were plaguing me with a vengeance as my body shouted, "I can't take any more. Enough is enough."

While casually driving with Andy into Baltimore City on a sunny January afternoon, a very strange thing happened.

"Andy, a big black magic marker is scribbling in my left eye, and I'm having trouble seeing. I'm going to pull over so you can drive. I need to get to an eye doctor quickly."

A few calls later, I identified an eye specialist in the Johns Hopkins system near my residence and made a call.

"Come to my office immediately."

Andy called Terry. We picked her up and headed for the doctor's office. As I sat in the ophthalmologist's chair I prayed and prayed, *What now, God? Show me what to do.*

"You have a tear in your left retina," the doctor told me. "You need to go directly to the Wilmer Eye Institute at Johns Hopkins Hospital downtown. It needs to be treated ASAP."

At Wilmer, a retinal specialist confirmed the diagnosis, and another doctor repaired the horseshoe tear with laser therapy. The procedure was relatively painless, and I was told to return in several days.

I returned to Wilmer three days later for more eye exams and additional laser therapy.

On February 14, at another follow-up visit, the doctor told me, "Today we are going to do laser-directed cryotherapy over the same area to permanently reattach the retina."

It seemed to take forever, and the longer it took, the worse I felt. Terry and Andy went to get the car, and an attendant wheeled me to the front entrance. I was trembling. The pain in my eye became unbearable.

"Wheel me back to Wilmer. Something is wrong."

I had an unexpected reaction to the procedure. They gave me pain medication, put me in an exam room, and waited until the discomfort passed before allowing me to leave the building. "Come back in a month," they told me.

On March 27, I was seen by the head of the department. I had no vision in my left eye.

"It takes a while for the vitreous to clear all of the dead blood cells that leaked into your eye," he told me. "Once it clears, your vision should be fine again. Come back in a month, and we'll check it again."

By early April, my vision was worse than ever, and outpatient surgery was scheduled for April 14 to remove the inner eye sac.

"We found and repaired several small blood vessel leaks behind the vitreous that were continuing to blur your vision," the surgeon said encouragingly.

I could see clearly again. I sang "Praise God from whom all blessings flow" all the way home.[1]

Currently, I have good vision in both eyes but still need glasses for reading. My skirmish with blindness was sobering. I am grateful I can see and have gained heightened empathy for those who can't.

I was knocked down but not knocked out. I could see. I had hope. I had God.

CHAPTER 47 — MEANWHILE, CANCER

Meanwhile, I had followed through on Terry's suggestion to contact Mercy Hospital for a second opinion on the suspicious spot detected by the earlier mammogram. The new radiologist ordered a biopsy.

Lord, this result is in your hands.

Time seemed stationary, but only a few days later I got the call—February 15, 2017.

"The result is positive for invasive ductal adenocarcinoma. I'm referring you to Dr. Friedman. He's an excellent breast cancer surgeon."

Dr. Friedman had been following Terry's case for decades. A few days later, he gave me more details about my tumor. "The tumor is small, 1.2 cm. Estrogen positive, progesterone positive, and HER2 negative. Stage 1A, meaning a low risk for distant recurrence at ten years. No radiation is needed or recommended. You have several surgical choices: lumpectomy, mastectomy ..."

"My bikini days are over," I told him. "I'm getting older. I don't want to have this surgery a second time. I'd prefer a double mastectomy now. Removing both breasts is the most practical choice for me."

He agreed.

I copied Jerry Bridges' poem in my journal on March 5, 2017:

> Lord, I am willing
> To receive what You give,
> To lack what You withhold,
> To relinquish what You take,
> To suffer what You inflict,
> To be what You require.[1]

On March 7, I had the double mastectomy, spent one night at Mercy, and returned to my apartment where Terry lovingly cared for me while I recovered, as I had helped her many years ago. During this procedure, the gynecologist also removed those two lymph nodes that had sounded the early alarm on my cancer.

I was left with what the surgical nurses call *dog ears*—large amounts of excess flesh under both arms. They looked grotesque, were extremely impractical for fake breasts, and made clothing look odd and feel uncomfortable.

On April 28, 2017, I made this journal entry:

> I wondered how long it would be before I shed a tear or two over these recent health challenges. Not when I got a cancer diagnosis; not before or after the double mastectomy; not while contemplating complete blindness (although this was very frightening); not even during the first four weeks of recovery from surgery.
>
> But by Thursday, I'd had enough. After intense discomfort from these pesky surgical drains and nagging pain across my chest during a four-hour car ride to Virginia to visit a friend and attend two conferences, a few tears appeared. At the end of a long tiring day, even Tylenol every four hours hadn't brought relief. Groaning with every breath, I carefully got into bed and the tears came.
>
> My friends heard the moaning and came to my bedside. Betty sang a comforting old hymn,

and Terry prayed over me. After I calmed down, I gradually went to sleep for the night.

I once saw a greeting card tacked onto a kitchen corkboard that one sister sent another sister who was undergoing chemo for breast cancer. It said, "Never, never, NEVER, NEVER, never, never, never, never, NEVER, NEVER, NEVER, NEVER, never, never, never, never, NEVER give up."

In the morning, I remembered a familiar Bible passage penned by the apostle Paul:

Therefore, in order to keep me from becoming conceited, I was given a thorn in my flesh, a messenger of Satan, to torment me. Three times I pleaded with the Lord to take it away from me. But he said to me, "My grace is sufficient for you, for my power is made perfect in weakness." Therefore I will boast all the more gladly about my weaknesses, so that Christ's power may rest on me. That is why, for Christ's sake, I delight in weaknesses, in insults, in hardships, in persecutions, in difficulties. For when I am weak, then I am strong. (2 Cor. 12:7–10)

I can relate to the thorn analogy. I had two big drains like two giant thorns in my sides. Biblical scholars still speculate that Paul's thorn in the flesh was poor eyesight. Interesting, huh?

Now that I am in the same dreary state of lingering weakness, I have an opportunity to become strong by never giving up or never giving in to despair.

I'm not there yet, but I am plodding in the right direction.

Psalm 56:8 reminds me that God keeps a record of all my tears and records them in a book.

In God's house, there is a huge bottle of tears with my name on it attached to a big book, recording the events that produced each one. Amazing. Who else would or could care that much except for the God who unconditionally loves me? The book and the bottle of tears are not full yet, but one day I will be able to boast about all those tears and difficult moments and about how Christ's power was made perfect in my weakness.

Glorious and mysterious indeed!

Six weeks later, I was back at Mercy to see Dr. Collins, a plastic surgeon who agreed that revision plastic surgery was advised. I had bilateral mastectomy scar revision surgery on June 14. Although this procedure was not invasive like the first one, I still faced drainage tubes and another six weeks of recovery. The incision across my sides and chest was almost three feet long. I was not a happy camper.

Cassie flew up from Florida and spent the following week with me. I was grateful for her help.

On April 28, 2017, I made this journal entry:

I always admired school friends who were good at sports. I never was. I especially dreaded running any sort of race, however short. When I finished the course, I thought I was going to die on that very spot, gasping for breath, trying to hide my embarrassment. I was usually last, far behind everyone else on the course. Running was to be avoided at all costs.

I didn't have any physical endurance to speak of and wasn't very motivated to acquire any. I have come to regret that.

But I did endure two pregnancies and lengthy deliveries. I thought I was going to die both times, but the doctors patted my arm and reassured me that I was going to live through each and, obviously, I did.

And I have endured all sorts of other things. Heartbreaks, shattered dreams, losses of people and things dear to my heart. Over the years, I learned how to endure hard things out of necessity. I guess I did have choices to make in each situation, but giving up, succumbing to despair, or cursing God were never options.

Now, I am having to endure things I would avoid like the plague. Like the compression straitjacket around my midriff, shoulders to waist, to control post-surgical edema. It was confining to say the least. This week the surgeon said I could take it off because it wasn't helping. He said "You're just juicy. We don't know why."

"For the rest of my life?" I asked.

"Yes," he replied.

This cancer diagnosis, which will affect the rest of my life, one way or another, will continue to require a steely endurance. The kind of endurance that all the other trial runs have equipped me to survive. I doubted I was ever capable of this level of endurance. Maybe the old practice makes perfect adage is an idiom I need to reconsider.

The Bible puts it this way: "And let us run with perseverance the race marked out for us, fixing our eyes on Jesus, the pioneer and perfecter of faith. For the joy set before him he endured the cross, scorning its shame, and sat down at the right hand of the throne of God" (Heb. 12:1–2). May it be so in me.

CHAPTER 48—BRISTLECONE PINES

In 1969, on my first and only literal mountain top experience during the best week of my tumultuous life, I summited Mt. Princeton in Colorado near Young Life's Frontier Ranch. Wind chill at 14,000 feet reddened my cheeks, and the 360-degree panorama of mountain ranges, as far as the eye could see, aroused my soul.

There, I stumbled upon a scene that would come to guide the rest of my life. A chalky gray wooden cross with a carved message—"Be still, and know that I am God—Psalm 46:10"—was staked firmly near a small patch of deformed, weather-beaten bristlecone pine trees.

Recently, when sharing an ongoing inconsolable sadness with my sister Jessie, I couldn't find words to describe the feelings. Then I remembered the bristlecone pines. She immediately understood.

Bristlecone pines thrive in harsh environments where most trees and other vegetation can't survive. Near freezing temperatures, high winds at high altitudes, rocky dry soil, and short growing seasons develop their longevity, endurance, and resilience. Most roots are shallow, but several go deep, very deep. The deep ones keep the tree standing long after it is dead. Although their height is stunted, these pines are sturdy and can survive for millennia. For me, they illustrate resilience learned through the brokenness of my life.

The Bible verse chiseled on that lonely summit cross has been chiseled into my heart and mind over seven decades (feels like millennia!). But now, as I stand on the summit of a resilient life transformed by the breathtaking vista of countless mountain ranges strewn with brokenness, I am in awe. My soul is still aroused, and I have learned how to live and thrive by being still,

Knowing that he is God.

That when you've had enough,

God is enough.

CHAPTER 49—THE CHAPTER I DIDN'T SEE COMING

In writing this memoir, retracing my fifty-six-year-old friendship with Joni was the most challenging task. Sifting through decades of dormant papers, letters, photos, memories, and emotions was daunting.

In October 2019, while piecing together a timeline of events from forty years earlier, I discovered Joni's decision to leave Maryland, abruptly ending our business and ministry partnership, wasn't as sudden as I had always believed. It had evolved during the months of filming the *Joni* movie (August 1978 through January 1979) as many influential, visionary, and godly leaders offered to come alongside her to encourage, support, and expand the impact her testimony would surely have around the world once the movie was completed.

For forty years, I had assumed her flight for freedom was sudden and impetuous.

Was I mistaken then or now?

After all, neither of us had chosen to talk or write about the events that had permanently altered our lives. I kept reexamining the scraps of facts in front of me. There seemed to be no other explanation for the timeline I had reconstructed.

I was mistaken then, not now.

As this new reality sunk in, I thought *I've been blindsided again. A second time.* Old scenes of those sorrowful days replayed in my mind.

Numbness and grief overwhelmed me for several weeks. Then anger. Then depression.

Help me, Lord. Please release me from this. Speak to me. I don't know how to get beyond it.

I grabbed a Bible and found a quiet place on an outside terrace facing a gentle slope of trees and a meandering stream through my retirement campus. A familiar gentle breeze greeted me. I imagined I was back at the picnic table behind my house on River Road where I often retreated to sense God's presence. I would search the Psalms and trust that God would show up and speak to me.

I had picked up a New Testament.

OK. No Psalms. Now what? Philippians is a favorite book. I'll look there. It's familiar, comforting, and encouraging. I surely need all of that.

Paul wrote to the Philippians from prison in Rome. What a miserable dungeon that must have been. Making matters worse, he was told that a group of former friends and coworkers on the outside were stealing his thunder and vying for his converts.

As I read Philippians 1, the first three words of verse 15 grabbed my attention.

"It is true ... "

I sensed God's presence as if he were audibly saying, "What you discovered is true."

I kept reading, ingesting every word, and was grabbed again by verse 18—

"But what does it matter? ..."

There it was. The answer I'd been seeking. The truth I stumbled on doesn't matter in God's equation.

"...The important thing is that in every way ... Christ is preached. And because of this I rejoice."

Leaning back into the patio chair, my jaw unclenched, and my disheartened emotions subsided. The soothing balm of Christ's presence became almost palpable. With each passing day, internal peacefulness progressively replaced unrest.

What had happened to me those fateful days in 1979, and the lingering effects, had a purpose in God's perfect cosmic plan. They were all predetermined subatomic-like particles in his plan for my life and for the global proclamation of reconciliation with God through Jesus Christ. Forgiveness, redemption, and eternal life are good news. Free gifts for those who believe.

Because of this I rejoice. And I continue to rejoice.

Those profound losses were part of God's beyond Diana's ability to understand plan. They were for my benefit and yours. I wanted what had happened to me to have a deeper enduring benefit and blessing for Joni also. But how could it?

Seems impossible. But God, if you want Joni and me to talk, you've got to make it happen.

My emotional and spiritual healing continued through October and November.

Then, I heard that Joni was a last-minute addition to an event in Washington, DC, on December 14, 2019. She would be less than an hour's drive away from me.

I waited for the phone call I hoped would come.

"Joni and Ken are coming to Baltimore tomorrow to have lunch with you and visit for a few hours," a mutual friend told me.

There it was.

God, I shouldn't be surprised, but I am. Give me courage to risk saying the hard things. I feel unable.

Mid-afternoon in my apartment December 15, Joni and I sat alone for the first time in many decades. During our extended time together we dealt with old, previously unspoken memories. We unmasked secrets, gave explanations, filled gaps, expressed regrets, admitted mistakes, and the spirit of giving and receiving forgiveness passed between us. Emotions became tears, and tears became hugs as "I love yous" were repeatedly exchanged.

Our separate but similar stories of blessings through decades of previously unknown brokenness caused us to rejoice anew. Reconciliation of a once-broken but fully restored friendship had finally happened.

> The important thing is that in every way, Christ is preached.
> And because of this I rejoice (Phil. 1:18).

And this is what makes all the difference.

AFTERWORD

"Now I lay me down to take my sleep. I pray the Lord my soul to keep,"[1] is no longer a child's wishful prayer, but a veteran's benefit from finally quitting my first-responder job.

I tread the dawn on songs of praise now and lie down at nightfall with hymns of thanksgiving.

Not because all is well. It isn't. Far from it.

I continue to be broken and mended, crushed and restored. The triune God is purging the stubbornness of my self-control and pride layered with years of protests, lies, and denial. The less I resist, the more efficient and permanent the process.

Why then do I sing?

Because it is more than enough that God continually whispers to my spirit, "Beloved, I am here."

I am unconditionally loved by my Creator. His all-sensing Spirit within breathes and pulsates with every heartbeat. All my imperfections are forgiven and forgotten. He sees and feels every heartache and happiness. He understands every inner thought and emotion. I am his, and he is mine.

Just as the apostle Paul wrote: "And the peace of God, which transcends all understanding, will guard your hearts and your minds in Christ Jesus" (Phil. 4:7).

Finally, I'm at peace, securely nestled in the intimacy of his comforting embrace. He retrieves every broken piece of my heart and mind and binds them together again—better for the brokenness, stronger for the shattering, woven together by his providence.

The life I'm living, strewn with paradox, is not the one I dreamed of long ago. Yet, I consider it a kaleidoscope of the broken shards of my life forming an ever-changing thing of beauty. Each new day adds another dimension to this colorful pattern, making it more beautiful than the sum of all the yesterdays. I choose to cling to the future, not the past; to hope, not despair.

Why so hopeful? Because the end of my story is on the not-so-distant horizon. The promo trailer in anticipation of opening night is splendiferous. God's promises are new every morning, and great is his faithfulness.

My prayer is you too discover Jesus, the Good Shepherd who lays down his life for the sheep. Meet him in the mess of your life and learn how to not only survive but thrive as he tenderly beckons you to know him. Be sustained and empowered by his indwelling presence, one moment at a time.

> You will keep in perfect peace those whose minds are steadfast, because they trust in you. (Isa. 26:3)

May it be so for you.

NOTES

Chapter 3

1. John Fawcett, "Blest Be the Tie That Binds," 1782, in the Public Domain.

2. 20th Century Overcomers was a Bible Presbyterian Church Mid-Atlantic youth group, founded in June 1960 by Mrs. Allen A. MacRae and Mrs. J. Christian Buchan (from the Bible Presbyterian Church Archives of Rev. G. W. Fisher, Tacoma Bible Presbyterian Church, Tacoma, Washington).

Chapter 5

1. Elisabeth Elliot, *Through Gates of Splendor* (Wheaton, IL: Tyndale House Publishers, 1981).

Chapter 7

1. In 1962, the Christian Admiral Hotel was acquired by the Christian Beacon Press, headed by the Rev. Dr. Carl McIntire, for use as a Bible study and conference center. See Joyce Jones, "A Hotel's Many Lives," *New York Times*, August 21, 1994, NJ-13, https://www.nytimes.com/1994/08/21/nyregion/a-hotel-s-many-lives.html.

2. Shelton College was a private, Christian, liberal arts college located in Cape May, New Jersey. See Margaret G. Harden, *A Brief History of the Bible Presbyterian Church and Its Agencies* (Bible Presbyterian Church, 1967), 138–139, https://archive.org/details/briefhistoryofbi00marg/page/138/mode/2up.

Chapter 14

1. John Newton, "Amazing Grace," 1772, in the Public Domain.

Chapter 15

1. The Institute in Basic Youth Conflicts was officially founded in 1974 by Bill Gothard, minister, speaker, and writer. Informal seminars and self-published materials initially appeared in the late 1960s. His fundamentalist teaching encouraged Bible memorization, respect for parents, self-esteem, family, dating, purpose, and forgiveness. See "IBLP History," Institute in Basic Life Principles, accessed March 17, 2021, https://iblp.org/about-iblp/iblp-history.

Chapter 16

1. Seymour Kopf, "Man About Town," *Baltimore News American*, February 8, 1973, 2-C.

Chapter 31

1. Phoebe Palmer Knapp, composer, Fanny Crosby, lyricist, "Open the Gates of the Temple," 1903, in the Public Domain.

Chapter 32

1. William Backus and Marie Champion, *Telling Yourself the Truth* (Minneapolis, MN: Bethany Fellowship, 1980).

2. Charles Wesley, "And Can it Be?" 1738, in the Public Domain.

Chapter 35

1. Thomas Ken, "Doxology," 1674, in the Public Domain.

Chapter 38

1. Ken, "Doxology."

Chapter 44

1. Presbyterian Church in America, *Report of the Ad-Interim Committee on Divorce and Remarriage to the Twentieth General Assembly* (St. Louis: PCA Historical Center, 1992), 292.

Chapter 46

1. Ken, "Doxology."

Chapter 47

1. Jerry Bridges, *Transforming Grace* (Colorado Springs: NavPress, 2008), 213.

Afterword

1. John Cotton, *The New England Primer* (Boston, 1777; Aledo, TX: WallBuilder Press, 2001), 32.

ABOUT THE AUTHOR

Diana Mood is a "Granny," Encore Navigator, international creative developer, apostolic visionary, entrepreneur businesswoman, writer, speaker, trainer, missions, and disability advocate. Born in Baltimore, MD, she graduated with a BA in Speech & Theater, Secondary Education, University of Maryland Baltimore County in 1971; MA in Counseling and Psychotherapy, Loyola University, Barltimore, MD, in 1990.

For forty plus years, she has mobilized and trained trainers in ESL, disability ministry, and community development. She has co-authored three books, two disability training manuals, and many blog posts and newsletters.

She lives in a vibrant retirement community in Maryland. Visit Diana's website, www.dianamoodauthor.com and sign up for her mailing list: DianaMood@dianamoodauthor.com.

Diana would love for you to write a review and post it on Amazon, Goodreads, and/or Barnes and Noble. Reviews help readers find good books to read on subjects they're interested in. A review needs to be no longer than a couple of sentences or a paragraph and are very much appreciated by Diana.